Gran Canaria

by Gabrielle MacPhedran

Gabrielle MacPhedran, journalist and broad-
caster, is the author of several guide books,
including AA *Essential Berlin*, AA *Essential
Canary Islands* and AA *Explorer Spain*. She is
a regular contributor to the *Daily* and *Sunday
Telegraph*, *The Times*, *Country Magazine* and
other periodicals. She lives in Surrey with her
travel-writer husband, Adam Hopkins.

Above: *view over the rooftops of Fataga*

AA Publishing

Above: *window in Mogán*

Written by Gabrielle MacPhedran

First published 1998. Reprinted Nov 1998, Mar 1999
Second edition 2000. Reprinted May 2001
Reprinted Apr 2002. Information verified and updated.
Reprinted Aug 2002; April 2003 and Sept 2003
Reprinted 2005. Information verified and updated.
Reprinted May 2005
Reprinted 2007. Information verified and updated.

© Automobile Association Developments Limited 2002,
2005, 2007

Published by AA Publishing, a trading name of Automobile
Association Developments Limited, whose registered
office is Fanum House, Basing View, Basingstoke,
Hampshire, RG21 4EA. Registered number 1878835.

Automobile Association Developments Limited retains the
copyright in the original edition © 1998 and all subsequent
editions, reprints and amendments.

A CIP catalogue record for this book is available from the
British Library.

All rights reserved. No part of this publication may be
reproduced, stored in a retrieval system, or transmitted in
any form or by any means – electronic, photocopying,
recording or otherwise – unless the written permission of
the publishers has been obtained beforehand. This book
may not be sold, resold, hired out or otherwise disposed
of by way of trade in any form of binding or cover other
than that in which it is published, without the prior
consent of the publisher.
    The contents of this publication are believed correct
at the time of printing. Nevertheless, AA Publishing
accept no responsibility for errors, omissions or changes
in the details given, or for the consequences of readers'
reliance on this information. This does not affect your
statutory rights. Assessments of attractions, hotels and
restaurants are based upon the author's own experience
and contain subjective opinions that may not reflect the
publisher's opinion or a reader's experience. We have
tried to ensure accuracy, but things do change, so please
let us know if you have any comments or corrections.

Find out more about
AA Publishing and the
wide range of travel
publications and services
the AA provides by
visiting our website at
www.theAA.com/travel

Colour separation by Keenes, Andover
Printed and bound in Italy by Printer Trento S.r.l.

A03021

Contents

About this Book

KEY TO SYMBOLS

✚ map reference to the maps in the What to See section

✉ address or location

☎ telephone number

🕐 opening times

🍴 restaurant or café on premises or near by

🚌 nearest bus/tram route

⛴ nearest ferry stop

ℹ tourist information

♿ facilities for visitors with disabilities

✋ admission charge

↔ other places of interest near by

❷ other practical information

► indicates the page where you will find a fuller description

This guide is divided into five sections to cover the most important aspects of your visit to Gran Canaria.

Viewing Gran Canaria pages 5–14
An introduction to Gran Canaria by the author
    Gran Canaria's Features
    Essence of Gran Canaria
    The Shaping of Gran Canaria
    Peace and Quiet
    Gran Canaria's Famous

Top Ten pages 15–26
The author's choice of the Top Ten places to see in Gran Canaria, listed in alphabetical order, with practical information.

What to See pages 27–90
The four main areas of Gran Canaria, each with its own brief introduction and an alphabetical listing of the main attractions
    Practical information
    Snippets of 'Did You Know…' information
    4 suggested walks
    3 suggested tours
    2 features

Where To… pages 91–116
Detailed listings of the best places to eat, stay, shop, take the children and be entertained.

Practical Matters pages 117–124
A highly visual section containing essential travel information.

Maps
All map references are to the individual maps found in the What to See section of this guide.
For example, Maspalomas has the reference ✚ 29D1 – indicating the page on which the map is located and the grid square in which the mountain is to be found. A list of the maps that have been used in this travel guide can be found in the index.

Prices
Where appropriate, an indication of the cost of an establishment is given by € signs:
€€€ denotes higher prices, €€ denotes average prices, while € denotes lower charges.

Star Ratings
Most of the places described in this book have been given a separate rating:
❋❋❋   Do not miss
❋❋   Highly recommended
❋   Worth seeing

Viewing
Gran
Canaria

Above: *the beach at
Las Palmas*
Right: *local inhabitants
of Barranco de
Guayadeque*

Gabrielle MacPhedran's Gran Canaria

Early Islanders

The word 'Guanche', literally 'man of Tenerife', does not, strictly speaking, apply to the aboriginal people of Gran Canaria, although it is widely used. The spirit of these early Canarios is everywhere and they have left their mark on the physical appearance, the names and sports of many present-day islanders. Even cave-dwelling has persisted, and pottery is still made exactly as it was in prehistoric days before the potter's wheel.

Most people come to Gran Canaria for its abundant sunshine and its golden beaches. They head for the south and the guaranteed rain-free resorts such as Playa del Inglés, Maspalomas and Puerto Rico. Here, the pleasures of sun and rest and recreation often prove so seductive that some never set foot outside their resort except to catch the plane back home. Thus they miss the one essential characteristic of Gran Canaria – its diversity.

Consider the geography: to the west, the island rises to cliffs of jagged black rock, pounded by a spume-laced sea. Among the northern hills, clouds can blot out the sun for hours at a time – an astonishment to southern habitués. Equally unexpected to some is the central range of volcanic peaks, the highest of which can attract snow in winter. From these rocky heights, forests of pine trees descend to hillsides spiky with euphorbia and prickly pear. The central valleys are lush and green, some of them extraordinarily fertile, with palms sprouting like feather dusters among mangoes, pineapple and papaya.

There is majestic landscape and rural tranquillity in abundance. But do not ignore the capital, Las Palmas, or the smaller towns. After decades of neglect by central government, greater local autonomy and European funds have resulted in a striking face-lift of the island and a growing self-confidence among its people.

Fertile Fataga, an inland village surrounded by rocky hills

Gran Canaria's Features

With an area of 1,532sq km, Gran Canaria is third largest of the seven major islands of the Canarian archipelago. The largest are Tenerife and Fuerteventura. Gran Canaria has the greatest population.

It is a circular, volcanic island which last erupted seriously about 3,000 years ago. The land comes steeply down from the high central peaks, with vast *barrancos* – dry water courses or ravines – running to the coast like the spokes of a bicycle wheel.

The capital city is Las Palmas, which is also capital of the province bearing the same name. This consists of Gran Canaria and the other eastern islands, Fuerteventura and Lanzarote. The western islands, including Tenerife, La Palma, Gomera and El Hierro, form the province of Tenerife. Together, since 1983, the two provinces have made up the Autonomous Region of the Canary Islands.

Position: in the Atlantic Ocean, 210km from the African coastline, 1,250km from Cádiz.
Population: 790,000, with 380,000 in Las Palmas.
Number of annual visitors: 2,800,000.
Highest point: Pico de las Nieves (1,949m).
Wettest part: the north; average annual rainfall 500mm.
Average temperature: summer 24°C; winter 19°C.
Flora: the range of altitudes ensures the presence of plants from almost every climatic zone.
Fauna: the largest mammal is the rabbit.

Placing the Name
The name 'Gran Canaria' first appeared on a Spanish map in 1339. The historian Pliny the Elder (AD 23–79) called the island 'Canaria', a possible reference to the large dogs (from the Latin *canis*, 'dog') which he reported living on the island. It is unlikely that the native canary – a small brown finch with a poor singing voice – had anything to do with the matter.

Below: *Columbus House, Las Palmas*
Bottom: *volcanic stone and brilliant flowers*

Essence of Gran Canaria

Golden sands and blue seas are the essence of Gran Canaria for most visitors. But there are increasing numbers of people who come here to windsurf, sail, fish, ride, play golf, mountain-bike, fly aeroplanes or paraglide. Walkers and botanists find the island irresistible. As for nightlife, there is enough choice of clubs, cabarets, pubs, discos and casinos to satisfy any taste, mainstream or alternative, and at any decibel level. But whichever way you choose to enjoy the island, those blue seas and golden sands are never far away.

The wide, man-made beach at Puerto Rico, ideal for family holidays

THE **10** ESSENTIALS

If you only have a short time to visit Gran Canaria, or would like to get a really complete picture of the island, here are the essentials:

• **Watch the sunset** over the sea from the lighthouse at Maspalomas (➤ 46–47). Anglers cast their lines from the rocks, shadows deepen among the dunes, children trail home across wide sands after a sundrenched day.

• **Take a boat trip** from Arguineguín (➤ 42) or Puerto Rico (➤ 60) to Puerto Mogán (➤ 48), last resort village on the west coast, for a view of the island from the sea.

• **Walk in the Tamadaba pine forest** (➤ 72) with soft pine needles underfoot and undergrowth of cistus and thyme. Look down to the harbour at Puerto de las Nieves (➤ 83), far below, and across the sea to Mount Teide on Tenerife.

• **Linger in the sun** at a terrace café in the Parque Santa Catalina (➤ 38), in Las Palmas. Watch the locals play chess and dominoes at outdoor tables.

• **Make a weekend visit** to the Jardín Botánico Canario in Tafira (➤ 22). Bridal parties come in droves to be photographed in this verdant setting.

• **Visit the ancient religious site** of the island's aboriginal people at Cuatro Puertas (➤ 79). Look from the top of the windswept hill to imagine a time before the Spaniards arrived.

• **Have a coffee** in the lounge of the hotel Santa Catalina (➤ 101) in Las Palmas. All celebrity visitors to the island stay here, including King Juan Carlos.

• **See a Canarian wrestling match**, or *lucha canaria*, a team sport dating from pre-Spanish, Guanche times which sends the restrained Canarios wild with excitement.

• **Drive eastwards from Pasito Blanco** (➤ 52) on the old coast road at night for a sudden view, as you crest the hill, of the lights of Maspalomas and Playa del Inglés, like a shimmering blanket of stars.

• **Catch a performance** of Canarian folk singing and dancing back in Las Palmas at the Pueblo Canario (➤ 112) on Sunday morning.

Below: *beachside café at Maspalomas*
Bottom: *Tamadaba pine forest*

The Shaping of Gran Canaria

3000BC–AD1500
The island is inhabited by Cro-Magnon and Mediterranean-type Stone Age people, who wear skins, keep livestock and grow cereals. They have no written language.

1st century AD
First mention of the name 'Canaria', by the historian Pliny the Elder. He calls the archipelago 'The Fortunate Isles'.

13th century AD
Arrival of slaving expeditions from Europe.

1405
The Norman Jean de Béthencourt (➤ 14) fails in his attempt to conquer Gran Canaria for the Spanish throne.

1478
Juan Rejón founds the town of Real de las Palmas and begins subduing the island. The aboriginal people are led by two kings: Tenesor Semidan, who rules the west of the island from his base at Gáldar, and Doramas, chief of the east, who rules from Telde. Juan Rejón wins the first major battle.

A tile painting of Columbus putting his fleet in to repair on the Canary Islands

1480
Under the Treaty of Alcáçovas, Portugal renounces her claims to the Canary Islands.

1481
The Guanche king Doramas is killed at Montana de Arucas.

1482
The Guanche king Tenesor Semidan is captured, taken to Spain and baptised as 'Fernando Guanarteme'. He then joins the Spanish cause.

1483
Siege of Ansite. Most Canarios surrender. Others throw themselves off cliffs. The end of aboriginal resistance.

1492
Christopher Columbus puts in at Las Palmas for repairs to his ships on his first expedition to the New World. He returns on his second and fourth voyages.

1496–c1525
Intensive colonisation by Spaniards, Portuguese and Italians. Portuguese bring knowledge of sugar cane industry from Madeira and Italians provide capital investment.

Early 16th century
Growing prosperity for Gran Canaria from trade with the New World and cultivation of sugar cane brought from Madeira. The island is targeted by British, Dutch and Portuguese pirates.

18th and 19th centuries
After collapse of the

sugar trade, following competition from the New World, main exports are wine and cochineal (the insects which produce the dye are bred and fed on prickly pear). Las Palmas becomes an important refuelling port for transatlantic shipping.

Early 19th century
Growing resentment at Spanish control, encouraged by ideas of American Independence, French Revolution and colonial liberation in Spanish South America.

1820
Las Palmas becomes the capital of Gran Canaria.

1852
The Canaries are declared a free trade zone in an effort to boost the islands' economy.

1882
Work begins on the harbour, Puerto de la Luz, at Las Palmas.

Early 20th century
Intensive cultivation of bananas and tomatoes is undertaken.

1927
The Canary Islands are divided into two provinces, with Las Palmas de Gran Canaria as the head of the eastern province. Growing rural poverty results in illegal emigration to Latin America.

1936
General Franco visits Gran Canaria and, from here, announces the launching of the military coup which begins the

General Francisco Franco

Spanish Civil War (1936–9).

1950s
Canarians demand home rule.

1960s
Plans to develop the south of the island for tourism.

Bananas, still the principal crop in north Gran Canaria

1970s
Mass tourism arrives: tomato fields give way to hotels.

1975
Death of Franco.

1978
Spain becomes a constitutional monarchy under King Juan Carlos I.

1983
Spanish devolution leads to greater autonomy for the islands.

1989
Canary Islands become full members of the European Community (as part of Spain).

2002
Canary Islands introduce the euro.

11

Peace & Quiet

Astonishingly, for an island as populous and popular as Gran Canaria, peace and quiet are easy to find. Even in the main tourist resorts, hotel gardens are often planted like miniature tropical forests.

Fishing off the harbour wall at Puerto de la Aldea, the westernmost part of the island

The West Coast

The major road through the southern resorts abruptly leaves the coast at Puerto de Mogán (► 24) and shoots up the *barranco* into the mountains. Any beach from Playa de Mogán to Puerto de la Aldea at the island's northwestern tip is likely to offer solitude.

The beaches of Veneguera (sand), Tasarte (pebble) and Asno (rock and black sand) are all accessible on foot. It is possible to walk to Güigüí, the star of all remote beaches, but only for the hardy and sure-footed. Make a deal with a fishing boat from Puerto de la Aldea, Mogán or Puerto Rico to drop you there and pick you up. In the summer, there are regular boat trips to Güigüí from Puerto Rico.

Inland Reservoirs

The reservoirs of Chira, Soria and Cueva de las Niñas, in the west central part of the island, offer areas to relax beside the water but away from the coast. In some places you can swim off a small beach or dive off rocks. It is possible to hike between all three reservoirs.

Walks

Several hiking groups offer accompanied walks in the more remote parts of the island. These are usually run by foreign residents and are often oversubscribed. If you walk alone, make sure someone knows where you are heading and can raise the alarm if necessary.

Native Plants

Gran Canaria is a botanist's delight, with a wide variety of vegetation. Common endemic species include the *Pinus canariensis*, or Canary pine, which has the useful talent of regeneration after fire: new growth emerges from seemingly lifeless, charred bark. The hard wood of this tree, called tea, is used for ceilings and balconies. The rock rose (*Cistus symphytifolius*) and asphodel (*Asphodelus microcarpus*) grow in pine forests.

The extraordinary-looking dragon tree (*Dracaena draco*), closely related to the yucca plant, has become the botanical symbol of the Canary Islands. With branches like the legs of a stumpy grey elephant, ending in a spiky green crown, this primitive form of plant life is extremely long-lived. Early Guanches dried the red resin of dragon trees, which they used as medicine and as a dye, and islanders still use it as a cure for toothache.

The Canarian palm (*Phoenix canariensis*), found all over the island, is similar to the North African date palm but shorter, with larger, lusher leaves and a more perfect crown. The leaves are used for basket work and the trunk for making beehives.

Other endemic plants include the retama (broom), with yellow flowers in spring and summer; taginaste, which produces white or blue flowers in spring; verode, with pink or yellow flowers and tabaiba, a species of euphorbia, whose sap is used – with care – in popular medicine (it can cause temporary blindness). The cardón or candelabra cactus is a many-branched native euphorbia, technically *Euphorbia canariensis*. The sap is mixed with oil and used as a medicine.

Below: *the orchid house at Palmitos Park*
Bottom: *a vital source of water – the reservoir at Soria*

Gran Canaria's Famous

Jean de Béthencourt

Charged by Henry III of Castile with the task of conquering the Canary Islands, this Norman soldier (1359–1426) set out in 1402 with his lieutenant Gadifer de la Salle and took the island of Lanzarote, for which he was awarded the title 'King of the Canary Islands'. He next conquered Fuerteventura. However, the aboriginal people of Gran Canaria resisted him successfully, and he returned to France, where he eventually died.

Christopher Columbus

Genoan-born Christopher Columbus (1451–1506) persuaded the Catholic Monarchs, Ferdinand and Isabella of Spain, to sponsor his expedition to find a western route to India. Instead of the Orient, he found the New World. On his first, second and fourth voyages across the Atlantic, Columbus put in at Gran Canaria. The house where he stayed and the church in which he prayed lie in the Vegueta district of Las Palmas (➤ 26).

Jean de Béthencourt, the failed would-be conqueror of Gran Canaria

Name-dropping
Other names the visitor may encounter which are famous on the island but not widely known elsewhere, include:
Nicolas Estévanez y Murphy, poet;
Francisco Guerra Navarro (Pancho Guerra), novelist;
León y Castillo, engineer;
José Luján Pérez, sculptor and religious painter;
Tomás Morales Castellano, poet;
Alonso Quesada, poet;
José Viera y Clavijo, historian and natural historian.

Benito Pérez Galdós

Pérez Galdós (1843–1920), the 'Charles Dickens of Spain', was the youngest child in a family of 10, born to an army officer and his wife in Calle Cano 6 in the Triana district of Las Palmas. The house is now a museum (➤ 31). He studied as a lawyer in Madrid before becoming a full-time novelist and playwright. The island is extremely proud of Pérez Galdós, although he lived his adult life on the Spanish mainland. His best known works include *Episodios Nacionales,* a historical novel in 46 volumes.

Néstor Martín Fernández de la Torre

Artist Néstor (1887–1938) studied at the Academy of Fine Art in Madrid but always kept his roots alive in the city of his birth, Las Palmas. Many of his canvases – such as *Poema del Atlántico* – depict aspects of the island in a romantic, free-flowing manner. See his work at the Museo Néstor (➤ 36) in the Pueblo Canario. He painted the murals in the Teatro Galdós, shocking bourgeois sensibilities and, less controversially, designed the Tejeda parador.

Top Ten

Above: *colourful boats dot many fishing ports*
Right: *bust of Christopher Columbus*

1
Andén Verde

✚ 28B4

✉ Passes through the
districts of Mogán
(► 48), San Nicolás de
Tolentino (► 63) and
Agaete (► 76)

🍴 Fruit and fast-food van
in the Mirador del
Balcón car park (€)

🚌 101 San Nicolas
Tolentino–Gáldar

↔ Agaete (► 76)

*View of the vertiginous
coastline from the
corniche road of the
Andén Verde*

*Andén Verde, or 'Green Platform', is the name
given to a magnificent stretch of corniche road on
the island's northwest coast.*

Winding northeast along the cliff-face, the road offers
thrilling glimpses downwards, by way of plummeting rock,
to a vertiginously distant sea. Though the extent of the
Andén Verde is a little vague, this most exciting part of the
west coast effectively begins a short way north of San
Nicolás de Tolentino (► 63).

Running just inland for 6km or so from San Nicolás, the
road suddenly veers towards a gap in a hill-crest above the
sea. There is a small car park here, the Mirador del Balcón,
or Balcony Lookout Point. Though views from the car park
are very fine, it is worth descending the few steps to a
lower platform. From here, the rocks beneath, and the cliff
foot to the southwest, may be seen clearly. The cliff is
surmounted by a dramatic series of hills, each of them
terminating suddenly in a triangle of dark cliff. Each
successive triangle is a little lower than the one before,
their diminishing height marking the descent towards the
harbour at Puerto de la Aldea (► 56). The island of
Tenerife lies west across the water.

The road continues to the northeast, following the cliff.
There are one or two further spots where cars can pull off
the road, sometimes with difficulty, so take care. As the
Andén Verde draws to a close the road swings inland,
descending towards the little village of El Risco.

2
Barranco de Guayadeque

An enchanting canyon southwest of the airport, on the eastern side of the island, and a centre of population in pre-Spanish times.

Lying between the municipalities of Ingenio and Agüimes, this *barranco* is more praised by environmentalists than any other on the island. From the flat floor of the dry river bed, the walls of the ravine rise through green terraces of cultivation, through tall palms, eucalyptus and the soft green ping-pong bats of prickly pear, to lofty crags of red volcanic rock.

Many of the island's rarest plants live here, and much of the *barranco* has been designated a nature reserve. The 80 endemic species of flora found here include the *kunkelliela canariensis* and *helianthemum tholiforme*.

The aboriginal people who once lived in this fertile valley left behind hundreds of caves, natural and man-made, that served as homes, animal shelter and grain stores. The many burial chambers found here form an important part of the Guanche exhibits of the Museo Canario in Las Palmas (▶ 33). The area is little inhabited today, but the 50 or so inhabitants are probably the most direct descendants of this prehistoric aboriginal world. They still farm, keep animals and live in caves. They even park their cars in cave garages. In Roque, the one small hamlet on the valley floor, there are cave homes, restaurants and a cave church. The area's most famous restaurant, however, is the Tagoror (▶ 94), right at the end of the *barranco* in a series of caves overlooking the valley. The stream beds under the trees make a pleasant and popular picnic spot during the weekends.

✚	29E3
✉	Municipality of Agüimes: 30km south of Las Palmas, 28km northeast of Playa del Inglés
🍴	Several cafés in Barranco; Tagoror restaurant (€)
🚌	11 or 21 to Agüimes
♿	None
↔	Agüimes (▶ 42)
❓	Access on foot or by car from Agüimes or Ingenio (▶ 43)

Clearing the canyon's terraces for cultivation

3
Casa de Colón

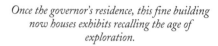

📍 35C1

✉ Calle de Colón 1, Las Palmas

☎ 928 31 23 73

🕐 Mon–Fri 9–7, Sat–Sun 9–3. Closed public hols

🍴 Near by

🚌 1, 2, 3

✋ Free

↔ Catedral de Santa Ana (▶ 32)

A celebration of the great explorer: the interior of the Columbus House Museum

Once the governor's residence, this fine building now houses exhibits recalling the age of exploration.

When Juan Rejón founded the city of Las Palmas in 1478, among the first buildings he erected was a residence for the governor of the island. When Christopher Columbus arrived on the island on his first voyage of discovery in 1492, he presented his credentials to the governor and lodged in his house. This house, much restored and refurbished, is now the Casa Museo de Colón.

The house is built around two courtyards of elegant stone, decorated with Canarian balconies of dense, dark tea pine wood. Twelve rooms on two floors contain the permanent exhibition; those dealing with the four voyages of Columbus to the New World are the most fascinating. A copy of the log of the first journey is left open at the page referring to the stop for repairs in Las Palmas. Given the direction of trade winds and ocean currents, the island was and is a natural stopping-off point in any journey westwards. Subsequent generations have found it easier to travel between the Canaries and the Americas than to go in the other direction to mainland Spain. Cultural, social and familial ties have always been supplemented by ties of trade, and in times of economic trouble, many Canarios have found it more natural to emigrate to Latin America than to go to the mainland.

Among the intriguing displays are nautical maps, as fanciful and crude as a child's drawing; navigational instruments, ingenious and inventive but looking hopelessly inadequate to the modern eye; the tiny ships, and the names of the seamen who manned them. All recall the magnitude of the explorers' task and the courage needed to fulfil it.

4
Cenobio de Valerón

This network of around 300 caves is one of the most important archaeological sites of the pre-Hispanic people of this island.

It was once thought that the complex, in a rocky cliff a few miles east of Santa María de Guía (▶ 85), was the abode of Guanche priestesses, or Harimaguadas, who served the god Alcorac; or that it housed young noblewomen in the period before marriage, when they were fed a calorie-rich diet in preparation for motherhood. Now, scholars agree that the caves were used as a fortified grain depository, indicating a high degree of social organisation.

The caves, under a red-yellow basalt arch like the upper jaws of a great fish, appear from a distance like a colony of swallows' nests, made up of round and rectangular chambers. They are reached by winding, steep stairs cut into the rock with the occasional platform.

Early writers described their astonishment on first seeing the Cenobio de Valerón, the round arch, the intricate complex of caves connected by steps and passages, and towers (now disappeared) at either side of the entrance overlooking the *barranco*. This was no mean achievement by people who had no knowledge of metal and used only stones and animal bones as tools.

Concerns for safety and the work of preservation have effectively put much of the complex out of bounds. It is no longer possible to clamber about inside the caves and explore the site. However, climbing up to this extraordinary place and seeing the evidence of the local 15th-century BC Stone Age culture is still a fascinating experience.

28C5

✉ Municipality of Santa María de Guía: 21km west of Las Palmas, 73km north of Playa del Inglés

☎ 928 21 94 21

🕐 Mon–Fri 9–2

🍴 None

🚌 103, 105 from Las Palmas

✋ Free, but guard is pleased with a small gratuity

↔ Santa María de Guía (▶ 85)

The caves tunnelled out of the cliff-face by the early indigenous islanders were originally built to store grain

5
Dunas de Maspalomas

✈ 29D1

✉ Maspalomas: 58km
south of Las Palmas,
6km south of Playa del
Inglés

🍴 Plenty of refreshment
places on and beside
the beach (€–€€€)

🚌 Faro de Maspalomas is
a busy bus terminal
with many services to
all areas. Bus 30 is a
frequent direct service
to Las Palmas

♿ None

↔ Playa del Inglés
(► 54–55)

❓ Don't feed the fish in
the *charco*. Left to
themselves, they eat
the mosquito larvae and
keep this section of
coast mosquito-free

*The changing contours of
a sculpted landscape as
the sun sets over the
Maspalomas dunes*

*Spectacular sand dunes, part of a protected nature
reserve, lie right in the middle of the busy tourist
resort of Maspalomas.*

Together with the Charco de Maspalomas – a freshwater
lagoon behind the beach – and its associated palm grove,
the dunes form an area of natural beauty and ecological
importance to the south and west of Playa del Inglés and
Maspalomas. Their sands, composed of fine ground shells,
can reach a height of 10m and are spread over an area of
328 hectares, ending at the mouth of the Fataga gorge.

Far from being composed of moving ridges shaped by
wind, like the better known parts of the Sahara, these
dunes are made up of what seems to be a host of sweetly
contoured hillocks and surrounding valleys. It is a mildly
surreal but loveable landscape.

When plans were launched in the early 1960s, by the
Count of Vega Grande, local aristocrat and landowner, to
start building tourist complexes on this coast, special pleas
were made that the dunes should be protected from

development. The luxury Hotel Grand Palace Maspalomas Oasis and the Maspalomas Golf Course were early lapses. But there are hopeful signs that this extraordinary natural asset, right in the centre of the greatest tourist concentration on the island, now has enough champions to protect it from further depredation. Meanwhile, the dunes are advancing at the rate of one metre a year from left to right in the direction of the lighthouse.

In the *charco*, over 20 different species of birds have been observed in the past, and there are indications that the lagoon is being used increasingly as a stopping point during migration.

Making tracks across the dunes at Maspalomas, with mountains ever present in the background

6
Jardín Botánico Canario

✝ 29E5

www.jardincanario.org

✉ Tafira Alta: 7km south of
Las Palmas, 53km
northeast of Playa del
Inglés

☎ 928 35 36 04

🕐 Daily 9–6

🍴 Jardín Canario
restaurant (€€)

🚌 301, 302, 303, 305. Ask
the driver to drop you
off at the gardens

♿ None

✋ Free

↔ Caldera de Bandama
(► 78)

❓ Occasional lectures

*Cactus in all its variety
is only one species of
endemic plant displayed
in the Jardín Botánico
Canario*

*This famous botancial garden in the Guiniguada
barranco reveals all that is spiky and smooth,
bizarre and beautiful of Gran Canarian flora.*

The garden was opened in 1952, with the aim of
preserving and displaying the many plant species endemic
to this island. Its first director was the Swedish botanist
Erik Sventenius, who did the preparatory groundwork of
finding and classifying, planning and planting – a task
assumed since 1974 by Dr David Bramwell.

The garden has two entrances, one at the top of the
150m-high *barranco* and the other at the flat bottom,
connected by paths and steps and taking you through the
different varieties of vegetation, planted at different levels.
Here is your chance to walk among Canarian palms and
the trees of the laurasilva forest that once covered this
island. The Jardín de las Islas displays all the most
important species of plants of the archipelago, and the
Cactus Garden has cacti from all over the world, with rare
examples from South and Central America. Endangered
species are carefully tended in two nurseries with the aim
of replanting them in their natural zones; there is also a
library for study and research.

At the top of the garden are the circular look-out point
and a white stone bust of historian and naturalist Don Jose
de Viera y Clavijo (the garden's official name is Jardín
Botánico Canario Viera y Clavijo). If you have managed to
get this far up from the bottom of the *barranco*, reward
yourself with some refreshment in the restaurant beside
the garden entrance.

7
Playa de las Canteras

This wide hoop of sand, over 3km long and protected by a natural rock barrier, is one of Las Palmas's most prized amenities.

Its position is extraordinary; backed by the hotels, shops and businesses of a major city, Las Canteras beach stretches in a golden curve, its comparatively shallow water warmed and sheltered from the wind by the presence of the inshore reef known as La Barra. A programme of improvements resulted in the planting of palm trees on the sands, and the re-building of a wide and attractive promenade, the Paseo de las Canteras, with attendant bars and restaurants, behind the beach.

Before mass air travel, visitors to Gran Canaria always arrived at Las Palmas by liner and tourism had its early beginnings in the north here, right behind Las Canteras beach. Older residents speak of a time when Las Canteras even boasted its own sand dunes, like Maspalomas, before the development of the town.

Summer weekends find the beach almost as crowded as those in the south of the island; its fans comprise foreign visitors and local Canarios who prefer the slightly cooler, occasionally cloudy days of the north, where the prevailing northeast trade winds form clouds as they hit the mountains. There is a good choice of hotel accommodation, pensions and apartments, many of them with sea views. As for restaurants and nightlife, visitors will find all they expect from a beach resort, combined with the usual offerings of a sophisticated modern city; but in the end, the beach itself is the star (▶ 39).

✛ 29E5

✉ Las Palmas

☎ Tourist Information Office at Parque de Santa Catalina ☎ 928 26 46 23

🍴 Cafés on and behind the beach (€–€€€)

🚌 1, 2, 3, 20, 21

🚢 Boats to Cádiz on Spanish mainland, jetfoil to Tenerife and ferries to all Canarian islands from passenger port

♿ None

↔ Vegueta (▶ 26)

The wide, sandy beach and the sheltered waters of Las Canteras, a step away from the city centre

8
Puerto de Mogán

🕂 28B2

✉ Municipality of Mogán:
81km southwest of Las
Palmas, 29km
northwest of Playa del
Inglés

🍴 Many cafés in resort
(€–€€€)

🚌 1, 32 from Maspalomas/
Playa del Inglés

🚢 Lineas Salmon boat to
Puerto Rico,
Arguineguín

↔ Mogán (➤ 48)

*Often referred to as Little Venice, Puerto de
Mogán is a low-rise resort in the southwest of the
island, complete with an attractive marina.*

Until the 1980s this was simply a fishing village at the
mouth of the Barranco de Mogán, providing shelter for a
community of hippies and bohemians as well as for local
residents. The hippies moved out – most unwillingly – as
the first concrete mixers arrived to create a new tourist
urbanización. Mutterings of rebellion against the continuing
massification of the coast were silenced here, however, as
apartments with prettily painted door and window
surrounds, pedestrianised streets, canals and bridges and,
above all, hibiscus hedges and roof gardens tumbling with
bougainvillea, began to appear in the new Puerto de
Mogán. Now, the resort is seen as an example of a tourist
building style which does not violate the natural landscape,
although more building inland is under way.

Puerto de Mogán has a curved, grey, sandy beach
protected by a breakwater, with sun beds and a beach
restaurant, tu Casa (➤ 96). The main focus here, however,
is the busy marina.

Throughout the day, passenger boats come and go
between Mogán and other southern resorts. There are
offers of fishing trips, sailing instruction and submarine
jaunts. Chic shops and restaurants always seem full.

Come evening, the day-trippers have gone and the
town assumes a quiet, reflective air. Then, if a breeze stirs,
you can hear the rigging rattling in the boats as you look up
to the grandeur of the mountains behind (➤ 56–57).

*Fishing harbour in the
purpose-built resort of
Puerto de Mogán*

9
Teror

Surrounded by hills, this is a beautiful showpiece town, as well as the spiritual heart of the island.

White houses with exposed grey stone, dark wooden balconies, turned and decoratively carved, enchanting small patios hidden behind stern doors – this is the style of Canarian vernacular architecture which is revealed at its best in Teror. Elegant and well preserved, the town also has the distinction of accommodating, in its splendid main square, shaded with ficus and pine, the Basilica de Nuestra Señora del Pino – the Cathedral of Our Lady of the Pine, the patron saint of Gran Canaria. On this site and in the branches of a pine tree, so legend goes, the Virgin appeared to the first bishop of Gran Canaria, Juan Frías, on 8 December 1492.

Decorated wooden balcony at Teror

The interior of the church is grand, with stone columns, a wooden coffered ceiling, a gilt *retablo* or altar-piece shaped like the stern of a ship and, above the altar, the 15th-century statue of the Virgin on a silver litter. The Virgin is traditionally dressed in the richest robes, regularly changed. She was also covered in a mass of precious jewels until 1975 when thieves made off with the treasure. They were never caught, and the incident is still a source of great anger and regret even to the most secular of Canarios.

Teror is an important place of pilgrimage to islanders all through the year but particularly during the fiesta of the saint on 8 September. Everybody converges on the town – on foot, donkey, car or cart – to offer prayers, fulfil religious promises, bring gifts of fruit and vegetables for the needy and – of course – to dance and sing the nights away. Every other week of the year, on Sunday mornings, a popular market is held behind the church (▶ 88).

✚ 29D5

✉ Municipality of Teror: 21km southwest of Las Palmas, 77km north of Playa del Inglés

🍴 Several cafés in town (€–€€€)

🚌 216 from Las Palmas

↔ Vega de San Mateo (▶ 90)

❓ 8 Sep is the feast day of the Virgen del Pino, celebrated throughout the island

25

10
Vegueta

35C1

Tourist Information
Office, Parque
Santa Catalina ☎ 928
26 46 23

Mon–Sat 8–2

Many cafés in area
(€–€€€)

1, 30 direct from
Maspalomas

Triana (► 34)

*Vegueta, the oldest part of Las Palmas,
contains a concentration of the most historic sites
of Gran Canaria.*

The Cathedral of Santa Ana stands near the spot Juan Rejón chose to found the Ciudad Real de las Palmas, the Royal City of the Palms, on 24 June, 1478. A few palms still flourish in the Plaza de Santa Ana, where children play among the pigeons and pensioners sit chatting on the benches. Two groups of bronze dogs, representing the animals after which the island is named (according to one theory) stand opposite the cathedral entrance.

The great explorer Christopher Columbus stayed in the house behind the cathedral now called the Casa de Colón (► 18). The church where he prayed before setting off on his voyages of discovery, the Ermita de San Antonio Abad, is also in the Vegueta, just behind the Casa de Colón.

The Vegueta is a place of surprising and delightful smaller squares – among them the Plaza del Espíritu Santo and Plaza de Santo Domingo. Stern mansions line the streets, often decorated with traditional pine balconies – for instance, Calle de los Balcones, Calle León y Joven, Calle Herrería and Mendizábal. The Montesdeoca restaurant, in the street of the same name (► 92), is a revelation both architecturally and for its outstanding Canarian food.

Do not miss the excellent Museo Canario for a glimpse of the life of the early aboriginal people of Gran Canaria. For modern life, a trip to the oldest of the city's markets, the Mercado Municipal, is highly recommended.

Pigeons strut in the palm-lined square in front of Santa Ana Cathedral, Las Palmas old town

What To See

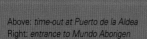

Above: *time-out at Puerto de la Aldea*
Right: *entrance to Mundo Aborigen*

27

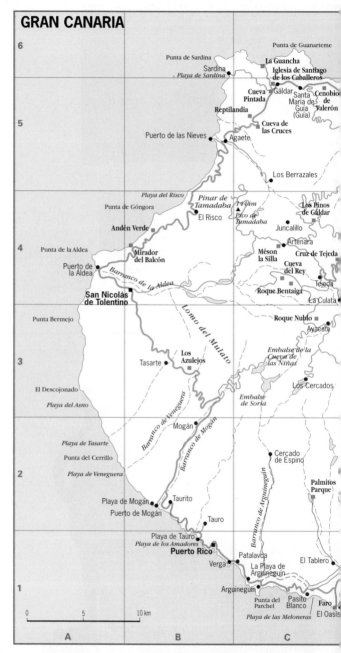

GRAN CANARIA

Punta de Guanarteme

Punta de Sardina
Sardina · **La Guancha**
Playa de Sardina **Iglesia de Santiago de los Caballeros**

Cueva Gáldar Santa **Cenobio**
Pintada María de **de**
Reptilandia ■ Guía **Valerón**
(Guía)
Cueva de
Puerto de las Nieves · ·Agaete **las Cruces**

Los Berrazales ·

Playa del Risco *Pinar de* 1444m **Los Pinos**
Punta de Góngora *Tamadaba* Pico de **de Gáldar**
■El Risco Tamadaba
Andén Verde ■ Juncalillo ·
· Artenara
Punta de la Aldea **Mirador** **Méson** **Cruz de Tejeda**
del Balcón **la Silla** · **Cueva**
Puerto de **del Rey**
la Aldea *Barranco de la Aldea* Tejeda·
San Nicolás **Roque Bentaiga**■
de Tolentino La Culata·

Punta Bermejo **Roque Nublo**■
Lomo del Mulato Ayacata·
Embalse de la
Los *Cueva de*
Tasarte · **Azulejos** *las Niñas*
El Descojonado *Embalse* Los Cercados·
Playa del Asno *de Soria*

Mogán·
Playa de Tasarte Cercado ·
Punta del Cerrillo de Espino
Playa de Veneguera **Palmitos**
Parque
Playa de Mogán·Taurito
Puerto de Mogán· ·Tauro

Playa de Tauro·
Playa de los Amadores **Puerto Rico**
Patalavaca · ·El Tablero
Verga· La Playa de
Arguineguín
Arguineguín· Punta del Pasito Faro·
Parchel Blanco· ·El Oasis
Playa de las Meloneras

0   5   10 km

| A | B | C |

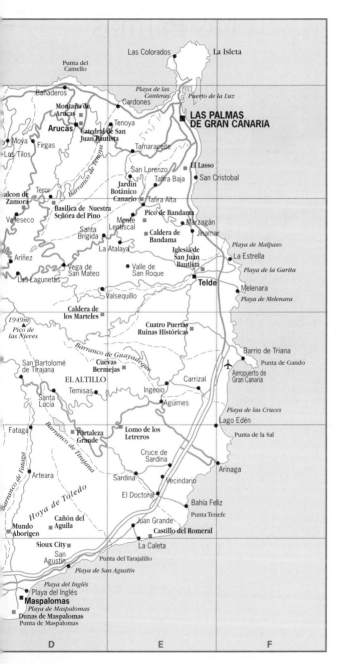

Las Colorados
La Isleta
Punta del Camello
Bañaderos
Playa de las Canteras
Cardones
Puerto de la Luz
LAS PALMAS DE GRAN CANARIA
Montaña de Arucas
Tenoya
Arucas
Catedral de San Juan Bautista
Moya
Firgas
Tamaraceite
Los Tilos
San Lorenzo
El Lasso
Tafira Baja
San Cristobal
Barranco de Tenoya
alcon de Zamora
Teror
Jardín Botánico Canario
Tafira Alta
Basílica de Nuestra Señora del Pino
Pico de Bandama
Valleseco
Monte Lentiscal
Marzagán
Santa Brigida
Caldera de Bandama
Jinamar
Ariñez
La Atalaya
Iglesia de San Juan Bautista
Playa de Malpaso
La Estrella
Vega de San Mateo
Valle de San Roque
Telde
Playa de la Garita
Las Lagunetas
Valsequillo
Melenara
Playa de Melenara
Caldera de los Martelos
1949m Pico de las Nieves
Cuatro Puertas Ruinas Históricas
Barranco de Guayadeque
Barrio de Triana
San Bartolomé de Tirajana
Cuevas Bermejas
Punta de Gando
Aeropuerto de Gran Canaria
EL ALTILLO
Temisas
Ingenio
Carrizal
Santa Lucía
Agüimes
Playa de las Cruces
Fataga
Fortaleza Grande
Lomo de los Letreros
Lago Edén
Barranco de Tirajana
Punta de la Sal
Cruce de Sardina
Arteara
Sardina
Vecindario
Arinaga
Barranco de Fataga
Hoya de Toledo
El Doctoral
Bahía Feliz
Punta Tenefe
Cañón del Aguila
Juan Grande
Mundo Aborigen
Castillo del Romeral
Sioux City
San Agustín
La Caleta
Punta del Tarajalillo
Playa de San Agustín
Playa del Inglés
Playa del Inglés
Maspalomas
Playa de Maspalomas
Dunas de Maspalomas
Punta de Maspalomas

D
E
F

Las Palmas

Las Palmas, the largest city in the Canary Islands, lies like a long (14km) and narrow ribbon on the island's northeast tip, barred from the sea by a highway. There are four distinct zones of interest: Vegueta, Triana, Ciudad Jardín and Playa de las Canteras. Vegueta, the monumental historic centre, adjoins Triana, a commercial district with fine examples of *modernista* architecture, a style of flowing curves and curious shapes. Ciudad Jardín (Garden City) is a leafy suburb created by British merchants in the 19th century, where you will find the Parque Doramas; and a quick hop across town takes you to Parque Santa Catalina and the splendid beach, Playa de las Canteras.

> *'Not without reason is the chief town of Gran Canaria called Las Palmas, for so many groups and groves of palms, with such superb stems, are to be seen nowhere else in the archipelago.'*

HERMANN CHRIST
Spring Journey to the Canaries
(1886)

What to See in Las Palmas

CASA DE COLÓN ✪✪✪

Christopher Columbus stayed in this house (▶ 18) while waiting for ship repairs during his first voyage of discovery to the New World in 1492. Originally 15th-century, but rebuilt in the 18th century, the house is now an excellent museum. Highlights include a life-sized reconstruction of the poop of the *Nina*, copies of Columbus's early charts and instruments, and a copy of the 1494 Treaty of Tordesillas, which effectively divided the undiscovered world between Spain and Portugal. There is also some excellent material on the history of Las Palmas. A small collection of 16th- to 19th-century paintings is on show, loaned from the Prado in Madrid.

🕂 35C1
✉ Calle de Colón 1
☎ 928 31 23 73
🕐 Mon–Fri 9–7, Sat–Sun 9–3. Closed public hols
🍴 Near by (€–€€€)
🚌 1, 2, 3
💲 Free
↔ Catedral de Santa Ana (▶ 32)

Left and above: *façade and detail, Casa de Colón*

CASA MUSEO DE PÉREZ GALDÓS ✪✪

The birthplace of the Canarian novelist, playwright and social critic, Benito Pérez Galdós, is now a museum and study centre. Born in 1843 in this fine town house built around a tiny patio, Pérez Galdós pursued a distinguished literary career on the Spanish mainland. Although he studied the influence of the old Guanche language on contemporary usage while he was a student, the island never featured in his writing – much to the disappointment of his compatriots. Exhibits on the first floor include the author's books, furniture made to his own design, a portrait of him by Sorolla and a re-creation of his study in Santander. When the museum first opened in 1964, a local bishop warned that a visit to the home of such a rabid anticleric might constitute a mortal sin.

www.casamuseoperezgaldos. com
🕂 35C2
✉ Calle Cano 6
☎ 928 36 69 76
🕐 Mon–Fri 9–7
🚌 1, 11
💲 Free, conducted tour on the hour

31

🔲 35C1
✉ Plaza Santa Ana
🚌 1, 2, 3
🔄 Casa de Colón (▶ 18 and 31)

Diocesan Museum and Cathedral
☎ 928 31 49 89
🕐 Museum: Mon–Fri 10–4:30, Sat 10–1:30. Cathedral: daily 10–8; tower 9:15–6
💶 Moderate

Below: *green on grey: the cathedral behind palms*

www.caam.net
🔲 35C1
✉ Calle de los Balcones 9–11
☎ 928 31 18 24
🕐 Tue–Sat 10–9, Sun 10–2
🍴 Cafés/restaurants (€–€€€)
🚌 1, 2, 3
💶 Free

CATEDRAL DE SANTA ANA

A mixture of Gothic, Renaissance, baroque and neo-classical styles reflects the fact that, although this cathedral was begun in 1497, it has only recently been completed and cleared of scaffolding. The west front, designed by local architect, Luján Pérez, and completed in the early 19th century, faces the large, palm-lined square of Santa Ana and the two groups of bronze dogs which, some feel, gave the island its name (▶ 7). Because of building works, the cathedral is reached through the **Museo Diocesano de Arte Sacro** (Diocesan Museum of Sacred Art). Here there is a fine, if limited, collection of polychrome sculpture; otherwise the religious paintings and liturgical objects on display are generally unremarkable. The museum building and courtyard, however, are beautiful, and a real reward in themselves.

CENTRO ATLÁNTICO DE ARTE MODERNO (CAAM)

This sparkling white gallery, housed in a grand mansion in one of the most picturesque streets of the city, opened in 1989 and shows the work of contemporary, mostly Spanish, some Canarian, artists. This is a surprisingly effective modern environment in an antique setting. Exhibitions are varied; the director is the noted sculptor, Martin Chirino.

MUSEO CANARIO ✪✪✪

In this excellent museum, dedicated to the prehistory of Gran Canaria, we get a glimpse of the lives of the neolithic people who inhabited the island at the time of Spanish conquest. They were of proto-Berber, Cro-Magnon and Mediterranean stock, many of them tall and fair-haired. Exhibits show that they lived in caves, as well as stone houses. They kept livestock and grew cereal; they ground grain with millstones and used pestles and mortars. They mummified their dead – see the long gallery of skulls, skeletons and mummies wrapped in *junco* (cloth made of reeds) and goatskin. They were expert at leather and cane work and made fine pottery, without the benefit of the wheel. Although they had no written language, they left many examples of rock engravings depicting humans, animals and geometric symbols. The famous Painted Cave of Gáldar (➤ 80), closed to the public during conservation work, is reproduced in this museum.

The islanders were ruled by kings, or *guanartemes*, practised sports such as wrestling and cross-stick fighting (still popular among modern Canarios), and, according to contemporary accounts, they loved music and dancing. The first Europeans described the inhabitants as generous, simple and trusting. However, when it became clear that their visitors, armed with superior weapons (the Guanches had no knowledge of metal and had never seen a horse), were intent on invading and enslaving them, they resisted them with courage and skill. Indeed they kept up this resistance for most of the 15th century.

www.elmuseocanario.com
✚ 35C1
✉ Calle Dr Verneau 2
☎ 928 33 68 00
🕐 Mon–Fri 10–8, Sat–Sun 10–2. Closed public hols
🍴 Good cafés near by (€–€€€)
🚌 1, 2, 3
💷 Inexpensive

Palm fronds for the faithful outside Santa Ana Cathedral

MUSEO ELDER ✪✪

This excellent Museum of Science and Technology has over 200 exhibits – many of which are interactive – all labelled in English as well as Spanish. You'll find a fascinating approach to subjects such as mathematics, biology and technology. You can watch chicks hatch, go inside an F5 plane, explore sound and waves and learn about energy. The IMAX cinema has screenings in English.

www.museoelder.org
✚ 35B5
✉ Parque Santa Catalina
☎ 828 01 18 28;
🕐 Tue–Sun 10–8 (summer 11–9). Closed Mon and some public hols
🍴 Café in museum (€)
🚌 1, 2, 3
💷 Moderate (IMAX cinema extra)

Did you know?

It appears that the Guanches lost all knowledge of navigation and therefore did not travel between the islands. Boatless, they fished from the shore.

A Walk Around the Historic District

Distance
2.5km

Time
1½ hours strolling, four hours with visits to attractions

Start point
Parque de San Telmo
 35C2

End point
Plaza de Cairasco
35C1

Lunch
Hotel Madrid (€)
✉ Plaza de Cairasco 2
☎ 928 36 06 64
Alternatively many cafés and bars in market area

This walk starts at Calle Mayor de Triana, the shopping street that leads down to Vegueta, the old city. After visiting Vegueta, it returns to historic Plaza de Cairasco.

Walk south from the hermitage (ermita) of San Telmo on pedestrianised Calle Mayor de Triana. Note the art nouveau buildings starting at No 98. Finally, angle left at the statue of Juan Negrín. At the major highway, go one block left to Teatro Pérez Galdós. Return and cross over to the market (Mercado de Las Palmas), on the left. Continue on along Calle Mendizábal, then right up handsome Calle de los Balcones.

Here, the local and national artistic heritage is on display at CAAM (Centro Atlántico de Arte Moderno, ➤ 32).

In Plaza del Pilar turn right, following the east side of the Colón house. At the next small square, the Church of San Antonio Abad is to the right, and a few steps further down to the right is the Montesdeoca restaurant (➤ 92). Return and follow the north side of Colón house (entrance on left). Continue straight ahead, with the cathedral to your left, into Plaza de Santa Ana and turn left, passing the cathedral façade.

The cathedral museum (➤ 32) is 25m left at the next turning, in Espiritu Santo.

Retrace your steps 25m to the end of Espiritu Santo. Turn left into Calle Reloj and walk to Calle Dr Chil. Turn right.

The Museo Canario (➤ 33) is on the left.

Passing the Museo, continue 60m up Calle Dr Chil, then angle sharply back into Plaza de Santa Ana. From the cathedral front, exit left down Calle Obispo Codina. Cross the highway and go straight on into Plaza de Cairasco.

Here you can recover with a drink or lunch outside the Hotel Madrid, where Franco spent the night on the eve of the insurrection of the generals in July 1936.

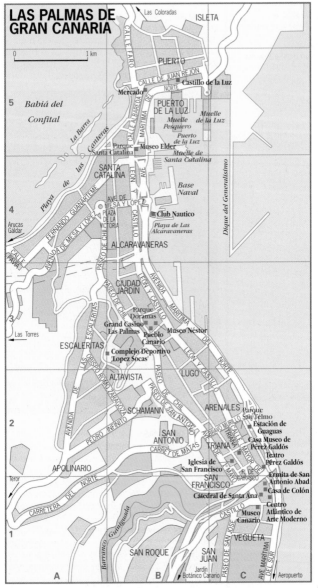

LAS PALMAS DE GRAN CANARIA

Las Coloradas

ISLETA

PUERTO

CALLE FARO

CALLE DE JUAN REJÓN

Mercado

Castillo de la Luz

NORTE

PUERTO DE LA LUZ

Muelle de la Luz

Bahía del Confital

Muelle Pesquero

Puerto de la Luz

CALLE ALBAREDA

AVE MARÍTIMA

La Barra

Parque Santa Catalina

Museo Elder

Muelle de Santa Catalina

Playa de las Canteras

SANTA CATALINA

AVE NORTE

Base Naval

Dique del Generalísimo

AVE DE MESA Y LÓPEZ

PLAZA DE LA VICTORIA

Club Nautico

Arucas Gáldar

FERNANDO GUANARTEME

AVENIDA DE MESA Y LÓPEZ

PASEO DE CHIL

Playa de Las Alcaravaneras

CALLE PAVÍA

ALCARAVANERAS

CIUDAD JARDÍN

LEÓN Y CASTILLO

AVENIDA MARÍTIMA

Las Torres

PASEO DE LAS ESCALERITAS

Parque Doramas

Grand Casino Las Palmas

Pueblo Canario

Museo Néstor

ESCALERITAS

Complejo Deportivo 'Lopez Socas'

ALTAVISTA

AVENIDA DE

OBISPO ROMO ZARAGOZA

PASEO DE CHIL

LUGO

LEÓN Y CASTILLO

SCHAMANN

PASEO DE SAN ANTONIO

ARENALES

Parque San Telmo

Estación de Guaguas

PEDRO INFINITO

SAN ANTONIO

BRAVO MURILLO

TRIANA

CALLE MAYOR DE TRIANA

Casa Museo de Pérez Galdós

Teatro Pérez Galdós

APOLINARIO

CARRET DE MATAS

Iglesia de San Francisco

SAN FRANCISCO

PL DE CAIRASCO

Ermita de San Antonio Abad

Casa de Colón

Teror

CARRETERA DEL NORTE

Catedral de Santa Ana

Museo Canario

CASTILLO

PASEO DE SAN JOSÉ

AVE MARÍTIMA DEL SUR

Centro Atlántico de Arte Moderno

Barranco Guiniguada

SAN ROQUE

SAN JUAN

VEGUETA

Jardín Botánico Canario

Aeropuerto

0 ___ 1 km

5

4

3

2

1

A

B

C

MUSEO NÉSTOR ★★

The life work of the island's most famous painter, Néstor Martín Fernández de la Torre (1887–1938) is displayed in this museum in the Pueblo Canario. His best known work, *Atlantic Sea Poem* (two series of four canvases), is a celebration of the island's ocean environment. Néstor was pre-occupied by the effect of modern development on the island, reacting with angry denunciations and positive projects for retaining all that is best in Canarian architecture. There are examples of both in the museum. The Pueblo Canario itself is part of his resistance.

Sculpture of a Guanche pole-vaulter in Parque Doramas

PARQUE DORAMAS ★

This shady park, in the middle of Ciudad Jardín, contains the Hotel Santa Catalina, the Pueblo Canario and the Museo Néstor. Doramas, after whom the park was named, was the last Guanche king of Eastern Gran Canaria. In 1481, on Montaña de Arucas, he challenged the Spaniards to single combat and killed his rival with a javelin throw, but was fatally wounded himself. The Spanish and Guanche forces then joined in battle, but it was soon over. This was the final act of armed resistance against the Spaniards. Many of Doramas's followers hurled themselves off the cliffs, an event commemorated in the wild bronze sculpture in the hotel garden.

---

www.museonestor.com
- 35B3
- Pueblo Canario
- 928 24 51 35
- Tue–Sat 10–8, Sun and hols 10:30–2:30
- Café in Pueblo Canario (€)
- 1
- Moderate
- Pueblo Canario (► 39)

- 35B3
- Ciudad Jardín
- Daily
- Café in Pueblo Canario and Hotel Santa Catalina (€–€€€)
- 1
- Free

A Walk Around the Parks and Gardens

This pleasant walk around the delightful old city of Las Palmas takes you to the Pueblo Canario (Canarian Village) (➤ 39), Parque Doramas (➤ 36), the Ciudad Jardín (City Garden) and the modern shopping centre, before heading northwards to the lively Parque Santa Catalina (➤ 38).

Start under the huge ficus tree to the southern side of the Pueblo Canario.

Within the Pueblo, the fine Museo Néstor (➤ 36) is to the right, the shops in front, and the outdoor café/restaurant to the left. Beyond the Pueblo is the Hotel Santa Catalina, which is worth a visit to admire its beautiful gardens.

Leave the hotel directly behind you, crossing the park (past the Doramas monument) to Calle León y Castillo. Turn left here, then second left up Avenida Alejandro Hidalgo. Take the first right into Calle Lord Byron, and go through Ciudad Jardín to the far side. Take the first left up Jose Miranda Guerra, then the second right into Leopardi and continue, angling right along Calle de Brasil. Take the third left (Calle Rafael Almírez), one block, to turn right on to Pio XII.

The route is now linear until its last stages, with many variations of neighbourhood (and changes of road name). The first stretch is dull, but after about 10 minutes the route reaches a produce market, to the right, and then intersects with the major shopping street, Avenida Mesa y Lopez (Corte Inglés and Marks & Spencer are both on your right).

Cross over the street and continue straight along it as it quickly becomes Calle Tomás Miller.

Playa de las Canteras (➤ 39), the town's fine beach, lies straight ahead.

The walk then turns right two blocks before the beach, up pedestrian Ripoche to Parque Santa Catalina with the excellent Museo Elder (➤ 33).

Distance
1.5km

Time
1½ hours strolling; 3 hours with attractions and shopping

Start point
Southern entry to Pueblo Canario
✚ 35B3

End point
Parque Santa Catalina
✚ 35B5

Lunch
Start with lunch at Bodegón in Pueblo Canario (€€)

37

🞦 35B5

✉ Santa Catalina

🍴 Many cafés around
(€–€€€)

🚌 1, 2, 3

ℹ Tourist Information Office
☎ 928 26 46 23

🔄 Playa de las Canteras
(➤ 39)

PARQUE SANTA CATALINA

The liveliest public space in Las Palmas, this park – which is really more of a city square – is surrounded by pavement cafés. Korean and Russian seamen mingle with African street-traders and tourists from northern Europe, while Canarians play chess and dominoes. Perfumeries and bazaar-like shops fill up the side-streets, which also act as a red light district by night. This is home to the Museo Elder, a museum of science and technology (➤ 33). You will find the city's main tourist information office in a traditional Canarian building at the corner of the square.

🞦 35C2

✉ Corner of Calle Bravo
Murillo and Avenida
Rafael Cabrera

🍴 Many cafés around
(€–€€€)

🚌 1, 11, 41

❓ Church open only during
services

PARQUE SAN TELMO ⭐⭐

A shady square full of tall palms and benches, this park is famous for its kiosk café, decorated in *modernista* style with ceramic tiles from Manises, and for its charming small church, the Ermita de San Telmo (patron saint of fishermen). The church, decorated with a little Canarian balcony, was rebuilt in the 17th century after destruction by Dutch pirates. Inside, there is a fine *artesonado* ceiling and a baroque retablo. On the west side of the park, a stern neo-classical building guarded by soldiers is the headquarters of the Spanish army in the Canary Islands. It was from here that General Franco announced his opposition to the Republican government on 18 July 1936 and broadcast a rallying call to his troops, thus beginning the Spanish Civil War from which he emerged the victor in 1939. A bus terminus and taxi-stand make this park an important communications point.

> ### Did you know ?
>
> *An exclusive club, founded in 1844 (when its president was Englishman Robert Houghton), has its home in the neo-classical Gabinete Literario, in the Plaza Cairasco in Triana. With its playful* modernista *decoration, this is one of Gran Canaria's finest buildings.*

🞦 35B4

✉ Alcaravaneras

🍴 Snack bars on beach (€)

🚌 1, 2, 3

PLAYA DE LAS ALCARAVANERAS ⭐

Las Palmas's second town beach after Las Canteras is a fine sweep of golden sand which has always suffered from its proximity to the port and the marina. Those suspecting the cleanliness of the water use the beach for sunbathing and beach football. Locals, self-styled 'fans of Las Alcaravaneras', would not go elsewhere.

PLAYA DE LAS CANTERAS ✪✪✪
The 3km-long Playa de las Canteras (➤ 23), sheltered by the inshore reef of La Barra, is the city's premier beach, which can become extremely crowded on summer weekends. The *paseo* behind the beach, with joggers morning and evening and walkers all day and much of the night, provides a fascinating indicator of a highly varied population. The major landmark of the area is the tall tower of the Sol Bardinos Hotel.

🕂 35A4
⊠ Santa Catalina
🍴 Cafés (€–€€€)
🚌 1, 2, 3, 20, 21
ℹ Tourist Information Office
  ☎ 928 26 46 23
↔ Vegueta (➤ 26)
❓ Boats to Spain and North Africa, jetfoil to Tenerife, ferries to Canarian islands

PUEBLO CANARIO ✪✪
The Pueblo Canario – the Canarian Village – is an attempt to preserve, re-create and display the best of Canarian architecture. A small group of buildings on the edge of Parque Doramas (➤ 36), based on the plans of the artist, Néstor Martín Fernández de la Torre (➤ 14), was erected after his death by his brother. There is a pretty courtyard, with outoor café tables, the restored Church of Santa Catalina, and a covered arcade of small shops selling Canarian handicraft – openwork tablecloths, musical instruments and Canarian knives with decorated handles.

🕂 35B3
⊠ Parque Doramas
🕐 Tue–Fri 10–8, Sun 10:30–2:30
🍴 Bodegón del Pueblo Canario (€€)
🚌 1
↔ Museo Néstor (➤ 36)
❓ Performances of traditional music and dance Sun 11:30AM

TEATRO PÉREZ GALDÓS ✪
Set on the edge of the busy carriageway that divides Triana from Vegueta, this theatre was designed by the architect Miguel Martín Fernández de la Torre and the murals (of Apollo and the Muses) painted by his brother Néstor in a style that shocked respectable theatregoers when they were first revealed. It is a haunt of the *haute bourgoisie* of Las Palmas.

🕂 35C2
⊠ Plaza de Stagno/Lentini 1 (view exterior only at present)
☎ 928 36 15 09
🚌 1, 11

Teatro Pérez Galdós

The South

In the south – which, for the purposes of this guide, extends from Gando airport in the east to Puerto de la Aldea in the west – the sun shines almost constantly. As a result the great resorts, many catering to mass tourism, are clustered here, including San Agustín, Playa del Inglés, Maspalomas and Puerto Rico. At first sight they look like brash, concrete cities in a barren landscape. Then, little by little, their appeal becomes clearer: Playa del Inglés, divided from Maspalomas by spectacular sand-dunes; Puerto Rico, lively and friendly; Puerto de Mogán, calmer and beautifully planned; Playa de Taurito, dramatic and floral. All different, but all dedicated to pleasure.

The interior is barely 20 minutes' drive from any coastal point. Ridges of cindery, volcanic rock separate deep ravines. White villages provide oases of palms and olives, and, in springtime, a plenitude of almond blossom. Once discovered, this region is never forgotten.

> *‘ There are two islands, ten
> thousand stadia from
> Africa; they are called the
> Isles of the Blessed. ’*
>
> PLUTARCH
> *Life of Sertorius*
> (1st–2nd century AD)

The South

What to See in the South

AGÜIMES ⭐⭐

In the east of the island, at the mouth of the Barranco de Guayadeque, is the town of Agüimes, surrounded by terraced hills. This administrative centre of an area famous for fruit and vegetables was once, from 1483 to 1811, the seat of the bishops of Gran Canaria, whose citizens enjoyed privileges not extended to the rest of the island. The imposing neo-classical church of San Sebastián is testimony to its early importance. A small square just above the church, surrounded by dark ficus trees, is a pleasant spot for civic events and festivities and the lively carnival in February.

The area surrounding Agüimes, dotted with caves and cave dwellings, supported an extensive population in pre-Hispanic times. Today the town boasts a famous team of Canarian wrestlers, Unión Agüimes.

ARGUINEGUÍN ⭐⭐

On an otherwise busy south coast, Arguineguín has for years been ignored by visitors – maybe due to the presence of a large cement factory on its outskirts. Now, hotels and apartments are being built for those who like the atmosphere of a lively little Canarian town. It has a good beach and, with an active fishing community, is famous for its fish restaurants. The extension to the motorway means that the town does not suffer as much from the former traffic mayhem.

North of the town, the Barranco de Arguineguín, a fertile gorge planted with papayas, passion fruit and avocados, rises from a flat valley floor towards the heights of the central mountains at Ayacata (➤ 66).

🕂 29E3
✉ Municipality of Agüimes: 30km south of Las Palmas, 28km northeast of Playa del Inglés
🍴 Bars and cafés in the square (€)
🚌 11, 21 from Las Palmas; 41, 52 from Maspalomas
↔ Ingenio (➤ 43)
❓ Thursday market. Feast of the Rosary, 7 Oct

Above: *a play on pastel in Agüimes*

🕂 28C1
✉ Municipality of Mogán: 66km southeast of Las Palmas, 14km west of Playa del Inglés
🍴 Bar Cofradía de Pescadores (➤ 94), Avenida del Muelle, offers good fish meals (€€) ☎ 928 73 59 56
↔ Puerto Rico (➤ 60)
❓ Tue & Thu market

ARINAGA ✪

A fast-growing, low-rise town with a lighthouse, a dark, rocky foreshore and a pretty Paseo Marítimo, Arinaga used to make its living from tomatoes and fishing. Now, many of its citizens are recent immigrants from inland villages who work in tourism-related industries. The coastline to the south is popular with dinghy sailors and windsurfers; the Bahía de Formas attracts migrating birds. A new harbour is being constructed but is not yet finished.

CASTILLO DEL ROMERAL ✪

This small, rather tatty, fishing village of low white houses is named after a castle which has long since disappeared. It is popular with those in search of simple but good fresh fish restaurants, many housed in former fishermen's terraced cottages.

INGENIO ✪✪

Ingenio is a large town and still growing. Its name means 'sugarmill' and recalls its early 16th-century history as a base for sugar production. The old town, spilling down narrow streets from the church of Our Lady of Candelaria, boasts some fine houses. Most visitors head straight for the northern suburb of Las Mejías and the **Museo de Piedras y Artesanía Canaria** (Museum of Rocks and Canarian Handicraft): it displays an indifferent collection of rocks but excellent handicraft, particularly the open threadwork or *calados*, and embroidery, *bordados*, for which this town and its neighbour, Carrizal, are famous.

> ### Did you know ?
>
> *Canarian wrestling – lucha canaria – is a competition between two teams of wrestlers dressed in T-shirts and shorts, and fought in a sand-covered ring. This is one of several sports in Gran Canaria with direct roots in Guanche tradition.*

Sidebar

✚ 29F2
✉ Municipality of Agüimes: 36km south of Las Palmas, 20km northeast of Playa del Inglés
🍴 Cafés in town (€–€€)
🚌 25, 52 from Maspalomas
🔄 Barranco de Guayadeque (➤ 17)

✚ 29E2
✉ Municipality of San Bartolomé: 42km south of Las Palmas, 14km northeast of Playa del Inglés
🚌 52 from Maspalomas

✚ 29E3
✉ Municipality of Agüimes: 27km south of Las Palmas, 31km northeast of Playa del Inglés
🚌 11 from Las Palmas, 52 from Maspalomas
❓ Fiesta of Virgen de la Candelaria in Feb

Museo de Piedras y Artesanía Canaria
✉ Camino Real de Gando 1
☎ 928 78 11 24
🕐 Mon–Sat 8–6:30. Closed Sun
🍴 Small refreshment bar (€)
♿ Free

Ingenio, a centre for handicrafts

43

A Drive Around the Island

This long tour around Gran Canaria offers a glimpse of resorts, of the island capital, Las Palmas, and of magnificent volcanic scenery.

From Playa del Inglés take the coast road (not the motorway) to Arguineguín (11km).

The route leads through desert-like terrain. After Arguineguín (➤ 42), there follows a string of the newer resorts, Patalavaca (➤ 52) and Puerto Rico (➤ 60), a mass of matchbox constructions. Tauro and Taurito lead finally to Puerto de Mogán (➤ 56–57).

Fishing boats lined up at Puerto de Mogán

Keep right up the fertile barranco for Mogán itself (8km). Continue on the main road for San Nicolás (➤ 63) and Puerto de la Aldea (➤ 56).

Distance
Approximately 176km

Time
6 hours' driving, with possible detours

Start/end point
Playa del Inglés
🔲 29D1

Lunch
El Dedo de Dios (€€€) (➤ 98)
✉ Puerto de las Nieves

ℹ It is possible to break the journey with an overnight stop at Hotel Los Cascajos (€) (➤ 103), behind the square in San Nicolás.
Be aware that petrol stations in this area close on Sunday afternoons

The Mirador del Balcón (Balcony Viewpoint, 11km from San Nicolás) yields magnificent cliff views, ushering in a thrilling corniche drive along the Andén Verde (➤ 16) to El Risco (10km). Take care – this road is not for the faint-hearted.

Just before Agaete (16km), turn left (0.8km) to Puerto de las Nieves (➤ 83), with its fragile monolith beneath the cliffs: el Dedo de Dios, the Finger of God.

Inland from Agaete, there is a possible diversion up the pleasing Agaete *barranco* and down again (20–30 minutes). Gáldar (➤ 80) and Santa María de Guía (➤ 85) are unappealing from the road but repay exploration on foot.

Take the new highway from Gáldar to Las Palmas (➤ 30–39) or the old coastal highway through Guía. Enter Las Palmas by the tunnel; turn right at the sea front on the inner-city coastal highway (signs for Sur or South).

From here, the motorway follows the unappealing coast to Playa del Inglés (23km).

The little village of Juan Grande lies on the road between San Agustín and Vecindario

JUAN GRANDE ✪

This small complex of church, manorial home and garden/palm-grove belongs to the de Vega Grande family. The family's extensive estates consisted mostly of dry land, good only for growing tomatoes. But in the late 1950s it was Don Alejandro del Castillo, Count or Conde de la Vega Grande, who launched, in San Agustín, the first tourist development of southern Gran Canaria. By the 1970s the San Agustín/Playa del Inglés/Maspalomas resort was firmly on the tourist map and Gran Canaria had become a year-round holiday destination for northern Europeans. Tourism now accounts for 80 per cent of the gross national product of the island.

LOMO DE LOS LETREROS ✪✪

The 'Ridge of the Inscriptions', in the Barranco de Balos, is a remarkable aboriginal site: a 300m-long rock face bearing incised sketches of the human form, and geometric patterns such as concentric circles, spirals and triangles. Much weathered over the years, it has also been considerably defaced. The etched shape of something resembling a boat is significant in view of the fact that, by the time they were conquered, the islanders had lost all knowledge of navigation and boating. Local environmentalists disapprove of open access. As with many of Gran Canaria's important archaeological sites, lack of funding and official neglect compound the problems created by graffiti-writers and souvenir-hunters. The site is closed to the public at the time of writing, but it is posssible it may re-open in the future.

✚ 29E2
✉ Municipality of San Bartolomé de Tirajana: 40km south of Las Palmas, 12km northeast of Playa del Inglés
🍴 Fish restaurants in nearby Castillo del Romeral (€)
🚌 30, 44, 60, 90 from Maspalomas; 1 from Las Palmas
↔ Castillo del Romeral (➤ 43)

✚ 29E2
✉ Municipality of Santa Lucía de Tirajana: 33km south of Las Palmas, 23km northeast of Playa del Inglés
🍴 Cafés in nearby Cruce de Sardina (€–€€€)
↔ Fortaleza Grande (➤ 68–69)
❓ For information on the site: Agüimes tourist office ☎ 928 12 41 83

45

🔲 29D1
✉ Municipality of San
Bartolomé de Tirajana:
30km southwest of Las
Palmas, 6km southwest
of Playa del Inglés

🍴 Cafés everywhere
(€–€€€)

🚌 Frequent service from
Playa del Inglés inlcuding
1, 30; 30 from Las
Palmas

🚕 Playa del Inglés
(➤ 54–55)

MASPALOMAS

Although the twin resorts of Maspalomas and Playa del
Inglés have virtually merged into a single tourist conur-
bation, Maspalomas still has a more up-market image, no
doubt due to its magnificent dunes and the early building
of luxury hotels around the oasis.

The lighthouse (*faro*) and the bus and taxi terminus
mark the western boundary of the resort. From here a
promenade runs past chic shopping centres, bars and
restaurants and ends at the Barranco de Maspalomas,
which, at this seaward point, is occupied by a fenced-off
lagoon (*charco*) with reed beds, pampas grass and resident
and migratory birds. The Sardinian warbler nests in the
tamarisk groves between February and June.
Environmentalists are making themselves heard in the
debate between developers and conservationists, particularly in relation to the dunes and the lagoon, and there is an
Information and Interpretation Centre behind the Hotel Riu
Palace in Playa del Inglés. Beach and dunes stretch east
from here to join the sands at Playa del Inglés.

To the west of the lighthouse the neighbouring luxury
resort of Las Meloneras has a sheltered bay, shopping mall,
and a luxury hotel designed in traditional Canarian style.

North of the lagoon, the *barranco* turns into a dry river
course with the prestigious 18-hole Maspalomas Campo
de Golf to one side. Estates of select apartments give way
to denser holiday accommodation, skirted by wide
avenues named after tour operators like Tui, Thomson and
Neckermann. The Faro 2 *centro comercial* is a circular
complex of shops, bars and restaurants. Amusement parks
mark the resort's northern edge.

*Holiday apartments
surround a pool in
Maspalomas*

What to See around Maspalomas

AQUASUR ★★

This water park, the biggest in the Canary Islands, is situated in the Barranco Chamoriscán, north of Maspalomas. Ideal for a family day out, it offers 29 slides, a slow river, wave pool, children's pools, a self-service café and large car park. The entry price covers unlimited use of all attractions.

🔲 29D1
✉ Mte León, Ctra Palmitos Parque km3, Maspalomas
☎ 928 14 19 82
🕐 Daily summer 10–6, winter 10–5
🍴 On premises (€)
🚌 45, 70 from Maspalomas
♿ Moderate

Lazy River at Aquasur

CAMELLO SAFARI DUNAS ★

North of the *charco*, camel safaris are offered through the sand dunes. Riders sit on either side of their ungainly beast, managed by Paco and his friends, then trundle off in a circle that takes half an hour to complete. A safari package for large, pre-booked groups includes a cup of mint tea (sitting cross-legged in a fake bedouin tent) followed by the camel ride, then a bus trip up the *barranco* and lunch at a ranch.

www.camellosafari.com
🔲 29D1
✉ Avenida Dunas, Isla de Lobos 70
☎ 928 76 07 81
🕐 Daily 9–4:30
🍴 Nearest café on beach (€)
🚌 Plaza del Faro, 29, 30, 32
♿ Moderate

HOLIDAY WORLD ★

Holiday World has something for all those who want a noisy, fun time. All the fun of the fair, with big wheel, rollercoaster, dodgems and roundabouts, plus bars, restaurants, bowling lanes, amuseument arcades, gym and two big discos.

🔲 29D1
✉ Carretera General Las Palmas
☎ 928 73 04 98
🕐 Fri–Sat 9–6, Sun–Thu 9–2
🚌 45, 70 from Maspalomas

PERLA CANARIA ★

On the road to Palmitos Park, next to Aquasur, is a pearl factory – part exhibition centre, part workshop and part gem store. Here you can watch the craftsmen at work and pick a pearl from the oyster tank to create your own custom piece of jewellery. The huge showroom has pearls, gold, semi-precious gems and gifts for sale.

🔲 29D1
✉ Carretera a Palmitos Park
☎ 928 14 14 64
🕐 Daily 9–7:30
🍴 Tropical tea garden (€)
🚌 45, 70 from Maspalomas

What to See in the South

✚ 28B2
✉ Municipality of Mogán:
88km southwest of Las
Palmas, 37km northwest
of Playa del Inglés
🍽 Cafés in town (€–€€€)
🚍 84 from Puerto Mogán,
86 from Maspalomas
↔ Puerto de Mogán
(➤ 56–57)

MOGÁN ✪

Mogán lies some 10km inland from the sea and its own harbour, Puerto de Mogán. The *barranco* running between the two is rich with tropical fruits; the slowly climbing road is lined almost continuously with hamlets. Numerous houses here are built in traditional rustic style, with large stones emerging through white rendering to create an attractive piebald effect. The little white town itself is comfortable and of some importance: it is from here that the whole district, including the coastline from Arguineguín to Puerto Mogán and even further west, is governed.

✚ 29D2
✉ Carretera de
Fataga
☎ 928 17 22 95
🕐 Daily 9–6
🍽 Café and
souvenir shop
on premises
(€€)
🚍 18 from
Maspalomas
💲 Moderate
↔ Arteara (➤ 66)

Model of an early island inhabitant in the Mundo Aborigen open-air museum

MUNDO ABORIGEN ✪✪

This open-air museum re-creates a Stone-Age settlement spread across the upper hillsides of the Barranco de Fataga. Life-sized figures of early Guanches occupy caves and stone-built houses, milling flour, cooking, performing a trepanning operation or participating in a religious ceremony. Their social hierarchy, their system of agriculture and knowledge of medicine – herbs, surgery, mummification – are clearly demonstrated and explained in Spanish, English and German.

Mundo Aborigen is based on the chronicles of the first invaders, who found the aboriginal people living in well-organised, close-knit groups. They are described as gentle and kindly, lovers of sport and music and redoubtable in battle.

The spirit of the Guanches is most strongly evoked in the beauty of the hillside and the views from this spot. To the west, dark striated gorges recede into the distance, and to the south, at the mouth of the *barranco*, lies the city of Playa del Inglés and the Maspalomas dunes.

Did you know ?

The early aborigines were great pole–vaulters – a useful skill in ravine country. Modern Canarios still use poles called lanzas or garottes, 3m long and ending in a steel point. Shepherds use them at work, but most are used in sport.

PALMITOS PARQUE ✪✪✪

Spread over 200,000sq m at the head of the Barranco de Chamoriscán, this park is one of the island's principal attractions. Exotic birds – 230 different species, many of them uncaged – include flamingoes, toucans, cranes, macaws, hornbills, peacocks and tiny hummingbirds.

Winding paths lead from one point of interest to another past a stream, a palm grove (there are 51 varieties among 1,000 palms), clumps of giant euphorbia, to a small island, home to a couple of white gibbons. The heated butterfly house has butterflies from all over the world, and the orchid house, said to be the first in Spain, is also spectacular. There are plenty of shady benches and cafés.

The park opened in the 1970s and has been regularly extended and improved. A 1,000sq m aquarium in a dramatic natural setting, with vast concave glass tanks set in rock surrounds, provides a panoramic view. Tropical fish from the Pacific region and the Amazon can be seen here.

A favourite with children is the parrot show, included in the entry fee. A well-trained troupe of macaws walks tightropes and rides bicycles to enthusiastic applause. Exciting birds of prey shows attract a large crowd.

🔳 28C2
✉ Barranco de Chamoriscán: 55km southwest of Las Palmas, 15km northwest of Playa del Inglés
☎ 928 14 02 76
🕐 Daily 10–6
🍴 Cafés and souvenir shops in park (€€)
🚌 Free bus services from Playa del Inglés, San Agustín and Puerto Rico
✋ Expensive
↔ Aquasur (➤ 47)
❓ Parrot shows every hour from 11AM. Birds of prey shows at 12:30 and 3:30

There is far more to see than palms in Palmitos Park, as this barranco garden reveals

In the Know

If you only have a short time to visit Gran Canaria, or would like to get a real flavour of the island, here are some ideas:

10
Ways to Be a Local

Smile – Canarios give an initial impression of shyness and reserve which disappears with the first smile.

Eat late. Lunch may not start until 2 and dinner not until 8, particularly away from the tourist resorts.

A Canario surveys the world with equanimity

Don't just rely on the menu in a Canarian restaurant. For best results, ask them what they are cooking.

Reserve beachwear for the beach if you do not want to look out of place.

Take a trip out into the countryside. Gran Canaria isn't just about beaches, bars and nightclubs, there's some beautiful inland scenery, too.

Take warm clothing if you are out for the day. Temperatures change fast.

Let your children be spoiled. Canarios love children.

Try speaking Spanish, however badly. It goes down well.

If the weather looks overcast, drive to another part of the island.

Don't get drunk: it's considered very bad form.

10
Good Places to Have Lunch

Balcón de Zamora (€€)
 Carretera a Vallesco km 8, Teror ☎ 928 61 80 42. Terrific views while eating good local dishes, including kid stew.

Café Madrid (€)
✉ Plaza de Cairasco 2, Las Palmas ☎ 928 36 06 64. Situated in the historic Hotel Madrid. Excellent value menu of the day.

Casa Montesdeoca (€€€)
✉ Montesdeoca 10, Las Palmas ☎ 928 33 34 66. Patio and ground floor of a restored mansion in the old town. Wonderful ambience, great food.

Casa Romántica (€€)
✉ Valle de Agaete, km 3.5, Agaete ☎ 928 89 80 84. Excellent international and Canarian food; great ice-cream and fruit.

Chipi-Chipi (€€)
✉ Avenida Tirajana 19, Ed. Barbados 1, Playa del Inglés ☎ 928 76 50 88. Unpretentious restaurant.

La Cantonera (€€–€€€)
✉ Avenida Tinamar, Vega

A camel safari makes its way through a barranco

de San Mateo ☎ 928 33 13 74. Canarian dishes in a museum of Canarian rural life.

Cofradía de Pescadores (€€) ✉ Avenida del Muelle, Arguineguín ☎ 928 73 59 56. A fishermen's co-operative with an island-wide reputation. Freshest of fish and seafood.

El Faro (€€) ✉ Puerto de Mogán ☎ 928 35 10 91. Lovely location in small lighthouse at the end of the fishing harbour. Excellent fish dishes.

Gran Buffet Las Camelias (€) ✉ Avenida Tirajana 15, Playa des Inglés ☎ 928 76 02 36. A self-service restaurant with a good variety at reasonable prices.

Hipócrates (€€) ✉ Calle Colón 4, Vegueta, Las Palmas ☎ 928 31 11 71. Vegetarian restaurant in the old town. Good service, pleasant atmosphere.

10
Top Activities

- Camel riding
- Deep-sea fishing
- Diving
- Go-kart racing
- Golf
- Horse-riding
- Paragliding
- Sailing
- Walking
- Windsurfing

For addresses and telephone numbers (► 114–15)

10
Top Souvenir Ideas

- Basketwork
- Black felt Canarian hat (*cachorro canario*)
- Canarian cigars
- Decorated Canarian knife
- Embroidery work
- Pottery, unglazed, hand-made
- Rum from Arucas
- Seeds of Canarian plants (in packets)
- Shepherd's woollen blanket
- Traditional stringed instrument (*timple*)

10
Top Views

- Ayacata in almond blossom (February)
- Bandama Golf Course, seen across the crater
- Fortaleza rock (ancient Ansite), from main road south of Santa Lucía
- Maspalomas dunes, from sky-diving parachute
- Moya, from the west side of the *barranco*
- Puerto de Mogán, from the sea
- Roque Bentaiga, from Artenara
- Roque Nublo, from most points in the island centre
- Tenerife, from Tamadaba pine forest
- Wild west coast, from Mirador del Balcón

Novice windsurfers take to the water

PASITO BLANCO ✪

- 28C1
- Municipality of San Bartolomé: 57km southwest of Las Palmas, 5km west of Playa del Inglés
- Restaurant in camping site behind marina at Pasito Blanco (€)
- 91 from Las Palmas and Playa del Inglés/ Maspalomas
- Arguineguín (➤ 42)

This attractive complex of houses, yacht club and marina lies in a sheltered bay just west of Maspalomas. Though it is private, the public may walk down from the GC500 highway into the resort to swim off the small beach to the right of the jetty, or dive off the rocks into Pasito Blanco's famously clear waters. Fifteen minutes' walk along the track to the west brings you to Playa de las Mujeres, where nude bathing is common and people occasionally camp out (illegally) at night. From here, another 30-minute walk brings you to the Playa de la Arena, but there are no shops or beach bars on the way.

A track in the opposite direction from Pasito Blanco, towards Maspalomas, brings you first to a fine sandy beach, Playa del Hornillo, and then to Las Meloneras, a wide, curved beach with a growing tourist development. The luxury Playa Meloneras Palace Hotel and a conference centre have already opened their doors, and a Canarian-style village, golf course and shopping centre are under way. The shining globe in the arid hills above Pasito Blanco, visible from the road, is the NASA space tracking station, the Estación de Seguimiento Espacial de Maspalomas.

A line-up of boats in the marina at the small southern resort of Pasito Blanco

PATALAVACA ✪

- 28C1
- Municipality of San Bartolomé de Tirajana: 68km southwest of Las Palmas, 16km west of Playa del Inglés
- 91 (as above)
- Arguineguín (➤ 42)

Patalavaca, literally 'Cow's Foot', is reputed to have the longest hours of sunshine on the island; it also offers a beach of light-coloured sand and flat rocks. Not surprisingly, this small resort is dense with steeply rising hotels and apartment blocks. The clientele is mostly Scandinavian. A coastal walkway connects Patalavaca with its neighbour, Arguineguín.

A Walk to Playa del Inglés

This walk follows the coastal promenade from San Agustín (► 62) to Playa del Inglés (► 54–55), and continues along the beach, around the Maspalomas dunes, to end at Maspalomas lighthouse. There is no shade on the beach; walk early morning or late evening and take plenty of water.

Start from the grey-sand beach at San Agustín, taking the much improved promenade to the right, past hotel gardens at first, then apartments.

Climbing a little above rocks, the path circles round to the beach of Las Burras, where a few fishing boats rest on the sands. The hotels of Playa del Inglés are now firmly in view.

Along the promenade, continue ahead to cross the wooden footbridge.

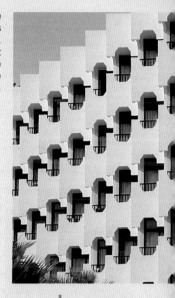

The bar on the right-hand side of the bridge, Kioska Las Burras, serves *bocadillos* (bread rolls with filling), salad and beer, plus wonderful freshly squeezed fruit drinks.

Passing the Europalace Hotel, the promenade ascends several flights of steps to follow the top of a modest cliff. At the centre of Playa del Inglés, it descends again to cross the only road along the route (Avenida de Alfereces Provisionales). Turn left along the road on to the beach, by now golden in colour, then follow the beach to the right.

Narrow at first, it soon expands into a wide wedge, with beach beds and beach bars and, towards the end, a nudist zone. Behind, the golden dunes now rise, not in long ridges but in individual hillocks.

Follow the fringe of beach around the dunes. Twenty minutes from the corner brings you to Maspalomas. Pass the freshwater pond to the right, then keep to the sea for the lighthouse.

San Agustín remains an attractive resort despite tourism

Distance
8km

Time
2½ hours

Start point
San Agustín
✛ 29D1

End point
Maspalomas
✛ 29D1

Lunch
El Señador beach bar (€), before the lighthouse

🔲 29D1
✉️ Municipality of San
Bartolomé de Tirajana:
52km south of Las
Palmas
🚌 30 from Las Palmas;
numerous local buses
ℹ️ Centro Comercial Yumbo
☎ 928 76 41 96
↔️ Maspalomas (➤ 46–47)

*The cave-shaped
Ecumenical Church of
San Salvador, in Playa
del Inglés*

PLAYA DEL INGLÉS ⭐⭐

The first sight of Playa del Inglés, as you swing south on
the motorway from the airport, is not reassuring. It has all
the marks of haphazard, unplanned and hastily assembled
hotels and apartments in a concrete sprawl.

Once inside the resort, the first-time visitor is likely to
get lost among identical streets with identical hotels. There
is no obvious town centre, no charming plaza with shady
trees and outdoor cafés of the kind that you will find in any
true Canarian town. Most of the life, apart from that
of beach and hotel, is concentrated in the rather grim
commercial centres (*centros comerciales*). These
are buildings of several storeys, often with one or two
below ground level, containing hundreds of small units
of shops, bars, restaurants and entertainments. They are worth visiting only in the
evening, when they become animated;
and even then, they may become too
animated for some tastes.

On the plus side of Playa del Inglés, the
sunshine is almost guaranteed, the beach
is splendid and the resort has plenty of
everything most tourists want: accommodation in every category, from *grand luxe*
to cheap *pension*, restaurants to suit every
palate and purse and representing every
national cuisine, with diversions – again, to
suit all tastes – for every hour of the day
and night.

It is also well-served with buses, a
legion of taxis and car hire agencies and
even a miniature train, so that moving
around, or out of, Playa del Inglés, is a
simple matter. In recent years a great deal
of money has been spent on planting
trees and flowers in public areas.

The nearest thing to a town centre in Playa del Inglés is
the vast, rectangular complex of the Yumbo Centrum with
the main Tourist Information Office at its southeastern
corner on Avenida de Estados Unidos. The Yumbo, the
largest of about 11 such centres in Playa del Inglés alone
(among them the Cita, Sandía, El Veril, Gran Chaparral), is a
vast bazaar of cheap clothes, leather, souvenirs, electronic
goods and perfumes. Of the many bars, restaurants and
entertainments on offer on its four floors, a substantial
number now caters for the gay community. The focus of
young nightlife (which begins after 10PM) revolves around
the *centros comerciales* like the Kasbah or the Metro

grouped around the Ecumenical Church of San Salvador, on Calle de Malaga. Cita Centre is also a popular venue.

In the early evening, the heart of Playa del Inglés is the long coastal promenade, the Paseo Costa Canario, which runs the length of the coast from San Agustín (▶ 62) to Maspalomas (▶ 46–47).

The district of San Fernando lies north of Playa del Inglés, bounded by the 812 highway and the GC1 motorway. This area is home to Canarian workers in the tourist industry. For the visitor, it provides the best chance of eating in local *tapas* bars and restaurants at local prices and – for self-caterers – of stocking up on groceries at prices lower than in the resorts. There is also a Canarian wrestling stadium beside the football ground.

Did you know ?

Most winter visitors to Playa del Inglés are German, some are Scandinavian. The British, and mainland Spaniards, tend to holiday here in the summer.

Modern Playa del Inglés, formerly tomato fields

+ 28A4
✉ Municipality of San
Nicolás de Tolentino:
76km southwest of Las
Palmas, 75km northwest
of Playa del Inglés
🍴 Good fish restaurants in
town (€–€€€)
🚌 38 from Puerto Mogán,
101 from Gáldar
⟷ Puerto de las Nieves
(► 83)

Above: *Puerto de la
Aldea, a picture of
tranquillity – until the
September fiestas*

PUERTO DE LA ALDEA ⭐⭐

The little harbour town of Puerto de la Aldea, sheltering
under a mountainous cape to the north, was long the only
practical means of reaching San Nicolás de Tolentino
(► 63), just inland. The *puerto* has a small selection of fish
restaurants and a promenade, with distant views of
Tenerife, leading south along the rocky beach. Behind,
among pine trees, is an extensive *merendero* (picnic area),
with tables and seating. Beyond, in the *barranco* bed, lies a
fresh-water pond, or *charco* – the finishing point of the
famous *bajada de las ramas* ('bringing down of the
branches'), celebrated each September. In a ceremony of
pre-Hispanic origin, local people would bring down palm
branches and beat the water with them in the hope of rain,
or possibly as a fertility rite. In 1766 the local bishop was
excommunicated for tolerating the *bajada*. Nowadays, it is
more of a water festival, with much excited leaping and
splashing in the *charco*, brandishing bunches of vegetation
and dancing to the band.

PUERTO DE MOGÁN ⭐⭐⭐

+ 28B2
✉ Municipality of Mogán:
81km southwest of Las
Palmas, 29km west of
Playa del Inglés
🍴 Cafés all around (€–€€€)
🚌 1 from Las Palmas, 32
from Playa del Inglés

This small but attractive town marks the present westerly
limit of tourist development on the island. Thoroughly
modern though it is, many day trippers come, often by
boat with the Lineas Salmón company, to enjoy its old-
fashioned, Mediterranean atmosphere. Puerto de Mogán
offers the gentle pleasures of strolling through floral lanes,
window-shopping, watching the bustle in the marina and

fishing harbour and eating at waterside restaurants.

If you continue strolling to the very end of the harbour, the views out to sea from the (not very high) terrace of the El Faro (The Lighthouse) bar/restaurant (► 95) make it a pleasure to linger over a drink.

Diversions include a trip in the Yellow Submarine (► 111), a genuine submersible (free bus service from major resorts). You can gaze at the splendours of the deep for 40 minutes out of your very own porthole. For the more active, the choice extends from diving (day or night), or learning to dive, to sailing (mono-hull or catamaran, with or without a skipper) and deep-sea sport fishing for marlin, tuna or barracuda. Shark fishing is also popular here. Trips usually last for about six hours and the price includes bait, tackle, rod and reel. Spectating passengers pay a reduced price.

Puerto de Mogán – the most westerly resort in Gran Canaria and, some say, the loveliest

Puerto de Mogán also has an excellent sandy beach. If you want some exercise followed by a quiet swim, you could walk along the road (looks closed, but is not) from the village to the next beach westwards at Veneguera. There are plans to build an *urbanización* there.

Did you know ?

Schools of whales and dolphins are a common sight in these waters. The best way to spot them is on summer boat trips.

To the east from Puerto Mogán to Puerto Rico, there is a series of beaches: Playa de Taurito, sandy with swimming pools, landscaped gardens and a smart *urbanización* or residential area; Playa del Cura, a growing *urbanización*, with much fresh construction under way, and a dark, sandy beach; and Playa de Tauro, a sandy beach, with the Guantanamo camping site straddling the road and a number of small houses to let. See also ► 24.

57

Food & Drink

Spaniards love eating out, and Canarians are no exception. Given the number of visitors here, it is no surprise that the island offers every kind of Spanish and European food. But Canarian food is rather different: country cooking, revealing a deep love for the island's own ingredients.

Main Dishes

Top of the list and found everywhere are *papas arrugadas* ('wrinkly potatoes'). These are small potatoes, boiled in their skins in water and coarse salt: 'saltier than the sea', says one local recipe book. They are eaten with a sauce called *mojo*. *Mojo verde*, or green *mojo*, is made with oil and vinegar, garlic, cumin, coriander and parsley; in *mojo rojo*, or red *mojo*, paprika is substituted for the coriander and parsley; and there is *mojo picon*, with a bracing dose of chilli. Taste before you dollop, especially the red varieties. These sauces are also served with fish and meat.

Less obvious to the visitor, since it is not often served in restaurants, is a form of cereal called *gofio*. Essentially this is any cereal – typically wheat or maize – toasted, then milled, and served either as a breakfast-type cereal with milk; moistened and made into little balls (a dumpling substitute); as a thickening in stews and soups, or as an addition to almost any kind of drink. This is the essential food of home and hearth. Most Canarians are addicted.

Other rustic dishes on the Gran Canarian menu include rabbit, usually served in stews, and hearty *sancocho*, a great favourite in bars and simple eateries. *Sancocho* consists of salt fish, usually in chunks, soaked and boiled, and served with *papas arrugadas*, *mojo* sauce and balls of *gofio*.

As may be expected, fresh fish is served in many places, especially in fishing villages. This, with or without

Paella, Spain's most famous dish, is always good value

mojo, is something that
should not be missed.
Cheese is also produced in
a number of villages, most
notably *queso de flor*
('flower cheese'), a light
goat cheese scented with
artichoke flowers.

Asparagus and avoca-
dos are grown in many
areas of the island.

Island Drinks

On an island where fruit is mostly tropical
and subtropical – mangoes and papaya are
common – the local fruit juice is well
worth tasting; and Gran Canaria also
boasts its own excellent mineral
waters.

Of other drinks, wine is produced in
small quantities, especially in the
Bandamas area, around Santa Brígida. A
number of *bodegas* can be found in and
around Monte de Lentiscal, and quality is said
to be improving. In San Bartolomé de Tirajana a
local liqueur called *guindilla* is made from the sour
cherry or *guinda*. A lemon-flavoured liqueur called
mejunje is made in Santa Lucia. More popular across the
island is local rum, *Arehucas*, made in Arucas on a base of
sugar cane. Canarian workers are very inclined to take a
shot of it at breakfast time.

Above: *fresh seafood is
always on the menu*
Below: *pork is usually
served as a casserole
or stew*

Canarian Desserts

On Gran Canaria desserts are not a culinary adventure.
Apart from *flan*, a custard pudding popular
throughout Spain, the local
speciality is *bienmesabe*
('how good it tastes').
Made from almonds
and honey, it is often
used as a sauce
poured over ice-
cream. Nougat and
marzipan are other
local products.

28B1

Municipality of Mogán: 72km southwest of Las Palmas, 20km west of Playa del Inglés

Choice of beach and town restaurants (€– €€€)

1, 91 from Las Palmas, 32 from Playa del Inglés/ Maspalomas

Mogán (► 48)

The marina at Puerto Rico, well known for watersports

PUERTO RICO

They say there will be no new building in this brash and thrumming resort because there is no room left – not for the tiniest hotel, nor the smallest apartment.

Puerto Rico grew up on the strength of its constant sunshine and the protection of encircling hills. The wide, man-made beach (with sand from the Sahara desert) shelves gently into the sea, making this a popular destination for families with small children. The western arm of the beach turns into a port, busy with offers of deep-sea-fishing, sailing, diving, windsurfing, jet-skiing and parascending trips. Another man-made beach, the fast-developing Playa de los Amadores, can be reached in around 20 minutes, by a clifftop path to the west.

Puerto Rico boasts a rarity among southern resorts: a town park, planted with ficus trees and palms, behind the beach. There is also a heated swimming pool, a bowling-alley, flood-lit tennis, *fronton* (the Spanish alternative to 'fives') and mini-golf courts, a water park and a *centro comercial* full of cheap shops and fast-food restaurants.

A Drive Around the South

This drive takes you from the coast to the central highlands through one *barranco*, and back down another.

Distance
Approximately 115km

Time
About 5 hours' driving

Start/end point
Playa del Inglés
➕ 29D1

Lunch
Take a picnic

Take the coast road to Arguineguín (➤ 42). At the roundabout behind the cement factory, turn right under the motorway for Cercado de Espina. Continue north into the barranco. At Cercado de Espina (12km), take the slip road right through the village. Soon, a steep zigzag climb begins, with wonderful views. At El Baranquillo Andrés (6km), a left turn is signed Mogán and Tejeda.

Another option is to continue onwards, into Soria village, with its reservoir and restaurants, then carry on to join the GC605 to Tejeda.

On the main route, turn left at Baranquillo Andrés. An asphalt road – probably best to use a 4WD vehicle – ascends through z-bends to meet the main (dirt) road ascending from Mogán. Turn right here for Tejeda.

The road soon runs close to a reservoir – Embalse de la Cueva de las Niñas – where there are agreeable picnic spots.

Continue 14km northeast through mountainous terrain for Ayacata. Turn right towards San Bartolomé de Tirajana; after 200m turn left (signed Los Pechos), climbing to pass Roque Nublo car-park. Continue through pinewoods, finally taking a right turn for Los Pechos, arriving at Pico de las Nieves.

There are more fine views of Roque Bermejo to the east.

Return to Ayacata and turn left to San Bartolomé. Follow signs for Fataga.

A hairpin descent takes you the into much-admired Barranco de Fataga, passing Fataga village and Arteara.

After a stiff climb out of the barranco, the road passes Mundo Aborigen (➤ 48) and continues to Playa del Inglés.

🕆 28D1
✉ Municipality of San
Bartolomé de Tirajana:
48km southwest of Las
Palmas, 4km northeast of
Playa del Inglés

Gran Karting Club
✉ Carretera General del Sur
km 46
☎ 928 15 71 90
🕐 Daily, summer 11–10,
winter 10–9
🍴 Café (€)
💰 Moderate

SAN AGUSTÍN ⭐⭐

Southern Gran Canaria's first shovelful of tourist concrete
was laid in San Agustín. Curiously, this resort, a step away
from popular Playa del Inglés (▶ 54–55), has never been
tarred with the brush of mass tourism. No doubt the
presence of the 4-star Melia Tamarindos Hotel and its
Casino have helped to maintain its up-market image. It is a
quieter and more sleepy resort with more of an appeal to
older people, less emphasis on younger nightlife and
more sophisticated restaurants.

The resort is cut in two by the GC500 highway, leaving
the hillside half connected to the beachside half by a series
of bridges. The main beach, the dark-sand Playa de San
Agustín, has the small Playa del Morro Besudo to its east
and Playa de las Burras to the west.

The three large hotels (including the Tamarindos), all in
Calle de las Retamas, are known for their splendid
gardens. Much of the other accommodation is in low-rise
apartments. San Agustín has its share of good restaurants,
though none are in the dismal *centro comercial*.

A short distance northeast of San Agustín, at a suitably
noisy juncture between the *carretera* and the motorway, is
the **Gran Karting Club** (▶ 111). Its 1,200m of track for
Go-Karts and Mini-Karts is the longest in Spain and its
clientele is of all ages and even caters for the under fives.
There is a pleasant lounge, café and games room and a
sunny terrace for spectators.

Above: *grey, sandy beach
at San Agustín*

SAN NICOLÁS DE TOLENTINO ✪

Sometimes known as 'La Aldea' or 'The Village', San Nicolás de Tolentino is tomato town. In a broad and dusty valley, well-settled in pre-Hispanic days, plastic greenhouses spread out in all directions. Towards the end of the season, tomato surpluses are dumped on wasteground, making brilliant splashes of colour. The town itself is mostly residential, with a cluster of shops round the church square and its restored Canarian-style church. Near by, in Tocodoman, is the excellent Cactualdea Park with impressive cactus plants and exhibitions.

🚩 28B4
✉ Municipality of San Nicolás de Tolentino: 71km southwest of Las Palmas, 70km northwest of Playa del Inglés
🍴 Cafés in town (€–€€€)
🚌 38 from Puerto Mogán
🔁 Puerto de la Aldea (➤ 56)

SIOUX CITY ✪

In the dry Barranco de Aguila, to the northwest of San Agustín and 300m from the beach, Sioux City is a Wild West theme park which has been created in the remains of an old spaghetti-western-style film set. Contributing towards the one-horse-town atmosphere are re-created saloons, church, bank, prison, bar and a sheriff's office. An action-packed show includes such diversions as knife-throwing, lassooing, pistol-shooting and, naturally enough, a bank robbery.

🚩 29D1
✉ Cañón del Aguila
☎ 928 76 25 73
🕐 Tue–Sun 10–5. Closed Mon
🍴 Cafés on premises (€€)
🚌 29 from Maspalomas
♿ Moderate
❓ Shows 12, 1:30, 3, 4:30

VECINDARIO ✪

Vecindario is a workaday town which stretches interminably along the main coast road. It is a modern creation born of rural depopulation and the demands of the tourist industry. Once a small village in a tomato-growing area, its size and relative prosperity have earned it the label *la ciudad de los Mercedes* – 'Mercedes city'. Street markets in Plaza San Rafael and Era de Verdugo sell excellent local produce.

🚩 29E2
✉ Municipality of Santa Lucía de Tirajana: 51km south of Las Palmas, 18km northeast of Playa del Inglés
🍴 Many cafés (€–€€€)
🔁 San Agustín (➤ 62)

Heroic civic sculpture marks the growing status of Vecindario

Central Gran Canaria

For those who love high mountains and volcanic landscapes, vast basalt columns rising solitary from rocky platforms, deep valleys, greenery, wild flowers in abundance – the centre has to be the place.

Pico de las Nieves is the highest point, more a mountain rim than a peak, looking down over the southeast. The free-standing Roque Nublo, a vast trunk of stone, rises almost as high, and looks west and southwest. Mountain villages, many with inhabited caves as well as houses, are gently domestic in atmosphere, white in colour, ancient in appearance. There are forests of Canarian pine, sometimes streaming with lichen, and echoing with woodpeckers. There are rocky hillsides dense with cistus, lavender, broom and thyme. There are short paths, long trails, rough roads and asphalt roads. Above all, there is a lofty landscape, offering drama and surprise at every turn.

> *'This Canaria is a land of mountains, trees, springs, streams, water wherever you look, and sharp-fanged cliffs.'*

MARIN DE CUBAS,
Historia de las Siete Islas de Canaria
(1694)

What to See in the Centre

ARTEARA ⚫⚫

Most visitors become aware of this tiny, fertile village, set in the beautiful Barranco de Fataga, only when they come here on camel safari. The camel ride skirts the village and by-passes one of the most interesting pre-Hispanic sites on the island: an ancient necropolis, containing hundreds of graves. Early Canarios used stone coffins, as well as caves, to bury their dead. Here, the stones lie in rubble spread over 2sq km of hillside at the southern end of the village.

ARTENARA ⚫⚫⚫

Dominated by a statue of Christ, this pleasant town is the highest on the island (1,219m). Every window, balcony or turn of the road offers thrilling views of the countryside – from its northern side towards the pinewoods of Tamadaba (► 72), and from its southern side across the wide valley in which the Roque Bentaiga (► 69) rises in solid splendour.

The surrounding landscape is riddled with caves of different sizes, some of them in continuous habitation since pre-Spanish times.

The biggest attraction here is the small, charming cave church, the Santuario de la Virgen de la Cuevita. The image of the Virgin and Child stands above an altar and pulpit hewn out of solid rock.

AYACATA ⚫

This mountain village, which serves as a staging post on the way to the highest point of the island from the coast, boasts a couple of restaurants, souvenir shops and some tremendous views – particularly in early spring, when the entire mountainside is covered in soft, pale clouds of almond blossom.

➕ 29D2
✉ Municipality of San Bartolomé de Tirajana: 55km south of Las Palmas, 10km north of Playa del Inglés
🍴 Nearest café in Fataga (€)
🚌 18 from Maspalomas
↔ Fataga (► 68)

Only the belfry indicates that this cave in Arteara is a church

➕ 28C4
✉ Municipality of Artenara: 49km southwest of Las Palmas, 91km north of Playa del Inglés
🍴 Good restaurants in town (€–€€€)
🚌 220 from Las Palmas
↔ Tamadaba (► 72)
❓ Fiesta of Santa María de la Cuevita, last Sunday in Aug: grand occasion with cycling competition and torchlit processions

➕ 28C3
✉ Municipality of Tejeda: 42km southwest of Las Palmas, 35km north of Playa del Inglés
🚌 18 from Maspalomas/ Playa del Inglés

This intricately carved stone cross marks the centre point of the island

CRUZ DE TEJEDA ⭐

At 1,450m, this intricate stone cross, set in a rather scruffy square full of stalls – with rather persistent owners – marks the notional centre of the island. The adjacent parador, which has seen better days, was built as a hotel in 1938 to a traditional design by Néstor de la Torre – a white house with exposed stone coigning and green woodwork. There are beautiful views of the surrounding countryside from the side of the parador, which is at present closed for repairs; it is not expected to re-open for visitors to stay in for the forseeable future.

🚩 28C4
✉️ Municipality of Tejeda: 37km southwest of Las Palmas
🍴 Food stands and restaurant in area (€–€€)
🚌 305 from Las Palmas; 18 from Maspalomas

EMBALSE DE SORIA ⭐⭐

This reservoir, built in 1971 at the head of the Barranco de Arguineguín, is the largest on the island, supplying water to the southern tourist resorts. It is also a popular swimming and fishing lake, fringed with Canarian palms standing among *taginastes* and *tabaiba*. Walkers who have laboured up the *barranco* often take a welcome break in the small village above the dam and sample the good local dishes and refreshing drinks, including freshly squeezed papaya juice.

The only thing that disturbs the general tranquillity is the weekend convoys of jeeps which climb past Soria to the next reservoir, the Embalse de la Cueva de las Niñas. To the east, the Chira reservoir completes a trio of artificial lakes in the centre.

🚩 28C3
✉️ Municipality of Mogán: 87km south of Las Palmas, 35km northwest of Playa del Inglés
🍴 In village (€)
↔️ Ayacata (➤ 66)

White walls and exposed stone create a typical piebald effect in this Fataga house

29D2

San Bartolomé de Tirajana: 60km south of Las Palmas, 16km north of Playa del Inglés

El Abaricoque (€) and cafés in village (€)

18 from Maspalomas/ Playa del Inglés

FATAGA ⊕⊕

This charming town of white houses with pink roofs, sitting on a knoll in its *barranco*, is much praised as an example of all that is loveliest in Canarian mountain villages – not least by its own inhabitants. They describe their home as *típico, pequeño, bonito* – 'traditional, small and pretty' – and themselves, with no false modesty, as *muy amables* – 'very kindly'. There is no arguing with any of that.

Fataga's reputation has spread and the village now has several bars and souvenir shops on either side of the main street. This is the thoroughfare connecting San Bartolomé de Tirajana in the centre and Playa del Inglés in the south. But the village itself, so neat, with cobbled alleyways, pretty houses and floral patios, and cocks crowing in clear, mountain air, seems timeless. It falls steeply into curved terraces like stacked plates and ends in a barranco floor bristling with palms. Above, the cliffs walls are made up of rocks like organ pipes.

The tiny church, planted around with shady trees, was built in 1880 and bears a plaque marking its centenary and commemorating those who built *tan magna obra* – 'such a great work'.

FORTALEZA GRANDE ⊕⊕

29D2

Santa Lucía de Tirajana: 42km south of Las Palmas, 28km north of Playa del Inglés

Cafés at Santa Lucía (€–€€)

Rising from the valley floor on the west side of highway GC65, to the south of Santa Lucía, this fortress-like rock formation was the scene, in April 1483, of the last resistance of the aboriginal people against their Spanish conquerors. The final nucleus of 600 men and over 1,000 women and children were urged to surrender by their former king, Tenesor Semidan, who had joined the Spanish side and been baptized as a Christian. Refusing to listen to him, many of his former comrades threw themselves off the cliffs, calling out the name of their god, Atis Tirma, as they fell to their deaths.

ROQUE BENTAIGA ✪✪✪

This dramatic monolith, raised like a rugged forearm with clenched fist, surges up to 1,404m from its own rocky massif, set in a broad valley. Visible from many points in the west and centre of the island, it is accessible by (very winding) road. For the aboriginal inhabitants of the island it was a sacred place and a scene of sacrifices. Bentaiga also made a most effective fortress, playing an important role in the resistance against the Spaniards. Its defenders, under cover of darkness, finally retreated from here to Ansite, where they congregated for their last stand. About 2km along the road from the Bentaiga/El Espinillo turning, in the westward extension of the massif, is the Cueva del Rey, a large, man-made cave, once painted, with side-chambers and floor holes.

🕂 28C4
✉ Municipality of Tejeda: 46km southwest of Las Palmas, 35km north of Playa del Inglés
↔ Roque Nublo (➤ 70)
❓ Half an hour's climb from the parking area on track signed to Bentaiga

Worn survivor of a greater mountain: Roque Bentaiga

The Roque Nublo stands sentinel over the small town of Tejeda

ROQUE NUBLO ✪✪✪

Though it is a little lower in altitude than the island's highest point at Pozo de las Nieves (1,803m compared to 1,949m), this spectacular basalt monolith dominates many views in the centre of Gran Canaria. It appears to be the final, irreducible core of a far higher volcanic mountain, formed about 3.5 million years ago, in the island's second great wave of volcanic activity, and long since peeled away by wind, water, snow and ice. One other, smaller rock, El Fraile, stands close to it. There is a footpath from the car park to the rocky plateau from which the Roque Nublo rises, and a footpath right round the little massif (➤ 71).

SAN BARTOLOMÉ DE TIRAJANA ✪✪

A quiet, agricultural town on the lip of a crater (the Caldera de Tirajana), San Bartolomé is the administrative head of the municipality which controls the tourist complexes of San Agustín, Playa del Inglés and Maspalomas. Climb its steep and sober streets, wander in its quiet squares and you will find a world far removed from the parched beaches of the deep south: a pastoral landscape of orchards and cultivated terraces.

San Bartolomé de Tirajana is famous for its local liqueur, *guindilla*, distilled from the sour cherry, or *guinda*, and combined with rum and sugar. The town is also well known for its wicker baskets.

A Walk Around Roque Nublo

This well-kept path makes a complete circuit of Roque Nublo and ascends to the plateau where it stands. It involves gentle descents and one stiffer climb, worth it for wonderful vistas, embracing deep valleys, glimpses of the ocean, the Bentaiga monolith and nearer rocky mountain crests.

Leave the car park by a small paved area, to follow the ridge directly ahead.

Views of Ayacata open out to the left, and there are fine views from the right-hand side of the ridge.

Near a finger of rock, the path begins to hairpin up; some 75m before the rock the path divides. Follow the right–hand path to make the circuit beneath Roque Nublo (left ascends directly to Nublo). The path now leads gently down (take care not to slip on pine needles) to the northwestern corner beneath Roque Nublo.

From here a ridge to the right leads to a castle-like rock outcrop (don't try to climb this), with surprising views of the valley and of Roque Bentaiga (add 20 minutes for the diversion).

Back on the main path, climb gently upwards, then more steeply.

There is a clear view of Roque Nublo from below, with the lesser rock, El Fraile, now in silhouette.

After 10 minutes, take a clear branch of the path left. Another 15 minutes of climbing brings you to a rocky ridge. Turn left here, with rough steps up to the rock plateau and the base of Roque Nublo. Return to the preliminary ridge and turn left and down, passing the point where the path first divided, and return to the car park.

Distance
6.5km

Time
Two hours; another 2 hours are added by starting and finishing the walk in Ayacata.

Start/end point
Car park, 2km north of Ayacata, steeply up, on road signposted Los Pechos
✚ 28C3

Lunch
Take your own supplies

Tejeda church, with Roque Nublo in the background

71

SANTA LUCÍA ✪✪

Visitors come in coachloads to Santa Lucía's major attraction – its museum, **Museo del Castillo de la Fortaleza**, in a former farmhouse now transformed into a pastiche of a miniature turreted castle. It contains an extraordinary jumble of old rocks, guns, stuffed birds, pressed flowers and amazing Guanche or pre-Spanish artefacts. These include pottery, tools, scraps of funerary clothes and other textiles made from reeds, astonishingly well-preserved, and a couple of skeletons. How such objects, part of the archaeological inheritance of the whole island, remain the property of a private individual – albeit a former mayor – is a puzzle. After the museum, visitors usually have lunch in the adjoining rustic-style restaurant, Hao (➤ 98).

Apart from these small diversions, which can create a traffic bottleneck, Santa Lucía is just another attractive mountain village presided over by its grand neo-classical church of white walls and dark grey stone. The business here is agriculture, particularly fruit-growing; the local liqueur is *mejunje*, made from lemons, rum and honey.

TAMADABA ✪✪✪

Eight kilometres from Artenara you will find the island's largest forest of Canary pines, much loved by walkers and picnickers, centred on the Pico de Tamadaba at 1,444m. There is a forestry station on the circular road leading round the mountain and an ICONA (national environmental agency) picnic site on the edge of the woods. There are splendid views from the summit down to the coast and, on a clear day, to Mount Teide on Tenerife.

🚩 29D3
📧 Municipality of Santa Lucía: 45km southwest of Las Palmas, 31km north of Playa del Inglés
🚌 34 from Agüimes or San Bartolomé de Tirajana

Museo del Castillo de la Fortaleza
📧 Calle Tomás Arroyo Cardoso
☎ 928 79 80 07
🕐 Daily 9–5
🍴 Restaurant in museum (€€)
👆 Inexpensive

🚩 28B4/28C4
📧 Municipality of Agaete: 57km west of Las Palmas, 99km northwest of Playa del Inglés
↔ Artenara (➤ 66)

The remains of a once extensive pine forest at Tamadaba

TEJEDA ✪✪

This peaceful and attractive mountain village is little visited because most people are *en route* to the tourist heart or centre of the island – the Cruz de Tejeda (► 67). Many young people have left Tejeda, once a thriving agricultural village, to find work in tourism-related industries; its major products now are sweets and cakes made from local almonds. At some point during the springtime, depending on the progress of the season, the town celebrates the Festival of Almond Blossom, Almendra en Flor, marking the beauty and commercial significance of the blossom.

✚ 28C4
✉ Municipality of Tejeda: 37km southwest of Las Palmas, 78km north of Playa del Inglés
🍴 Bar in village (€)
🚌 305 from Las Palmas; 18 from Maspalomas
↔ Cruz de Tejeda (► 67)

TEMISAS ✪✪

Temisas is a village half-way up a mountainside, famous for its rural architecture – white stone houses with pink tiled roofs, windows with wooden shutters, a little 18th-century whitewashed church with a belfry, a water mill and hillsides dotted with olive trees (Temisas is sometimes known as 'Little Jerusalem'). Like many inland villages, though, the problem here is depopulation, with the young leaving for coastal towns in search of almost any work that is easier than tilling terraces.

From here there are clear views down to a coast of plastic greenhouses, with the town of Arinaga (► 43) in the distance. The view is broken by the nearby bulk of a very solid rocky outcrop, unimaginatively named El Roque, rising from the plain beneath.

✚ 29D3
✉ Municipality of Agüimes: 35km south of Las Palmas, 33km north of Playa del Inglés
🍴 Bar in village (€)
🚌 34 from Agüimes
↔ Fortaleza Grande (► 68–69)

Above: *tucked away deep in the interior, the charming agricultural village of Tejeda*

73

The North

Before the mushroom-growth of the southern resorts, the cloudier, rainier, greener and far more fertile north of Gran Canaria was the place to be. Both of the island's pre-Hispanic kingdoms had their centres here: one in Gáldar, in the northwest, the other at Telde, in the northeast. The Spanish capital of Las Palmas, in the northeast corner, became one of the leading cities of the Spanish nation. Behind Las Palmas, the hills are lushly suburban, but the landscape is surprising, interspersed as it is with volcanic craters and cones.

Inland towns and villages such as Teror, Gáldar and Arucas offer fine old Canarian architecture. Overwhelmingly, the main crop is bananas. Because of the general sense of fertility and greenery, the *barrancos* appear softened, and some – Agaete above all – produce fine tropical and subtropical fruits.

> *'And often I forget all life's*
> *uncertainties thinking of*
> *these islands, the mountains,*
> *beaches, waves.'*

NICOLAS ESTÉVANEZ
poet (1838–1914)

What to See in the North
AGAETE ✪✪

Agaete stands at the mouth of the lush, green *barranco* of the same name. Its handsome old buildings, fanning out from a main square, with huge trees and a grand Canarian church, is one of the most charming spots on the island.

The church, the Iglesia de la Concepción, possesses a fine 16th-century Flemish triptych. This is shown during the Bajada de la Rama ('Bringing Down the Branch'), an ancient festivity celebrated in Agaete, Puerto de las Nieves (the town's little local harbour, 1km away) and in Puerto de la Aldea (➤ 56). On the lower side of town is a walled garden, the Huerto de las Flores, open to the public, venue for some of the town's cultural events. The 19th-century poet Tomás Morales wrote in these small and densely planted gardens.

The green and fruitful 7km-long Barranco de Agaete – producing mangoes and papayas, avocados, figs and coffee – eases the spirit after the harshness of so much of the island's volcanic landscape. There is one substantial tourist development, with privately owned houses and apartments, on the northern side of the valley. Elsewhere, ancient-looking villages run down on spurs from the *barranco* or cling to the steep slopes.

From the head of the *barranco*, there are fine views down towards the sea and upwards to the great bluff of Tamadaba, where Canarian pine forests fringe the top of a precipice.

✚ 28B5

✉ Municipality of Agaete: 37km west of Las Palmas, 89km north of Playa del Inglés

🚌 103 from Las Palmas

↔ Puerto de las Nieves (➤ 83)

❓ Fiesta de la Rama, 4 Aug: a Christianised festival with strong aboriginal roots

Above: *the prosperous little town of Agaete, in the northwest*

PLAZA SAN JUAN

ARUCAS ⭐⭐

Arucas is a lively, populous town with one extraordinary feature – the needle-pointed, frilly, neo-gothic Church of San Juan Bautista, so commanding in size and colour that it is often mistakenly called a cathedral. Built in a local grey basalt – *piedra azul*, or 'blue stone' – it was begun in 1909 and completed in 1977. The streets are unusually wide and straight, the result of a town planner's efforts in the mid-19th century.

Arucas used to be known as *la villa de las flores*, 'the town of flowers', and has fine subtropical gardens in the Municipal Park. Most of the greenery surrounding the modern town, however, is that of banana plantations, giving rise to a new description of Arucas: *republica bananera*, 'banana republic'.

Sugar cane and, even more so, the rum made from it, are also famous local products. An old-established distillery just beneath the town on the north side produces 50,000 litres of rum a day under the label *Arehucas* – the old Guanche name for the town. The distillery (▶ 108) and the **Museo del Ron** (Rum Museum) are both open to visitors.

Half a kilometre further on is the **Jardin de Marquesa**. Developed in the late 19th century, the garden displays 42 different types of palm trees, 400 different plants, bushes and trees and is well worth a visit.

To the northeast of town, the great volcanic cone of Montana de Arucas – scene of the death of the last great aboriginal freedom fighter, Doramas, in 1481 – offers views of La Isleta and the Bay of Las Palmas.

The Church of San Juan Bautista in Arucas

🔲 29D5
🔲 Municipality of Arucas: 18km west of Las Palmas, 70km north of Playa del Inglés
🍴 Cafés in town (€–€€)
🚌 205, 206, 210 from Las Palmas
↔️ Firgas (▶ 79)
❓ Feast day of St John, 24 Jun

Museo del Ron
☎️ 928 62 49 00
🔲 Era de San Pedro, 2
🕐 Mon–Fri 10–2. Closed Sat–Sun
💷 Free

Jardin de Marquesa
🔲 Carretera a Bañaderos
☎️ 928 60 44 86
🕐 Mon–Fri 9:30–12:30, 4:30–7; Sat 10–4
💷 Moderate

Did you know?
Cock-fighting is a popular activity on the island and Arucas is famous for its cock breeders. The fighting season runs from February to April.

✚ 29E4

✉ Municipality of Santa
Brígida: 10km south of
Las Palmas, 52km north
of Playa del Inglés. 2km
south of Tafira Alta,
reached via GC110 from
Las Palmas

🍴 Club de Golf bar (€€), Las
Geranios bar in village
(€€), opening times
erratic

🚌 311 from Las Palmas

🔁 Santa Brígida (▶ 84)

Above: *tracks lead down
to the farm at the bottom
of Bandama crater*

Right: *a cool seat in
Firgas*

CALDERA DE BANDAMA　　　★★★

The *caldera* or crater of Bandama forms a perfect bowl,
1km across and 200m deep, with no way out at the
bottom. Its steep but gentle-seeming slopes are made up
of dark grey ash, but the floor of the crater is patchily
fertile, containing a single farm with chickens and goats,
figs, oranges, palms and potatoes. The farmer, Juan, is
something of a celebrity. You can walk down into the
crater (about one hour) from the tiny hamlet of Bandama,
taking a path past the church. Take care, though, as the
steps soon peter out. Bandama, named after Dutchman
Daniel van Damm, who arrived in 1560 and planted vines
here, has a small bar which serves excellent roast pork and
red wine.

There are superb views from the
immediately adjacent Pico de Bandama
mirador (574m), the peak itself being a
large pimple on the volcanic rim. The
mirador is popular with coach parties
during the day and courting couples at
night, with some resulting wear to the
crater's upper slopes.

On the seaward side, there are lofty
views over the two Tafiras (▶ 86) and
to Las Palmas. On the west side of the
crater is the Club de Golf Bandama, the
oldest golf club in Spain, founded in
1891 by the British community who
settled in Santa Brígida and the neighbouring Tafiras. The club moved from
Las Palmas to this marvellous site on
the edge of the crater in 1956. The
accompanying Hotel Golf Bandama,
comfortable but seriously sporty, is
owned by a naturalised Spanish Swede
and patronised mostly by
Scandinavians, Japanese and the local
upper classes.

CENOBIO DE VALERÓN (▶ 19, TOP TEN)

CUATRO PUERTAS ●●
Cuatro Puertas (Four Doors) was a major religious site, used for worship and sacrifice by the aboriginal people of northeastern Gran Canaria. It comprises four cave openings, leading into a single large chamber. An open space in front was presumably ceremonial. The site is close to the summit of a windy hill, Montana de Cuatro Puertas. From here, you see that the whole hill is part of the otherwise vanished rim of a volcano.

✚ 29E3
✉ Municipality of Telde: 19km south of Las Palmas, 35km northeast of Playa del Inglés
🍴 None on site; bar in village below (€)
🚌 35 from Agüimes or Telde 🦽 Free

CUEVAS DE LAS CRUCES ●
Five kilometres north of Agaete on the Gáldar road, Cuevas de las Cruces consists of a number of adjoining rock chambers originally inhabited by the Guanches, one with a chimney. Nowadays, they contain a good deal of litter. The corner is awkward – take care entering and especially leaving the car park in front of the little complex.

✚ 28C5
✉ Municipality of Gáldar: 34km west of Las Palmas, 86km northwest of Playa del Inglés
🚌 103 from Las Palmas/ Gáldar 🦽 Free

FIRGAS ●
Pleasant little upland Firgas, 'capital' of the smallest municipality in Gran Canaria, is famous throughout the archipelago for its natural spring water: the bottling plant 5km out of town bottles 250,000 litres a day. In the town, whitewashed houses stand round a circular grey fountain. Firgas is also an agricultural community, producing bananas, cereals, fruit, watercress and yams.

✚ 29D5
✉ Municipality of Firgas: 25km west of Las Palmas, 78km north of Playa del Inglés
🚌 201, 202 from Las Palmas; 211 from Arucas

Interior of the church of Santiago de los Caballeros in Gáldar

GÁLDAR ✪✪

The most historic of all Guanche towns and now the centre of a banana-growing area, Gáldar shelters from the sea behind the near-perfect volcanic cone of La Montaña de Gáldar. It has an excellent covered market (famous for handicrafts and local produce) in the main street and a fine square, Plaza de Santiago. The church, with its wide neo-classical façade unusually built in a pale fawn-coloured stone, stands on the site of the palace of the former Guanche kings. The town also boasts a monument to Tenesor Semidan, the last king of Gáldar (Calle Guariragua), unveiled by King Juan Carlos I of Spain in 1986. The one-storey town hall on the corner of the square is a building of real charm in the best Canarian-Hispanic style. A dragon tree, planted in the patio in 1718, practically bursts through the walls.

A road runs out of the square for 200m, soon descending to an archaeological park, still under construction. This contains the famous Cueva Pintada (Painted Cave) of Guanche times (a model can be seen in the Museo Canario, Las Palmas: ► 33). Discovered by chance in 1873, it is elaborately decorated with squares, circles and triangles in red, black and white. The cave was closed to the public in the 1970s and remains so while work continues.

Did you know ?

Early Canarios worshipped the sun, which they called Alcora, or Alcorac, kneeling to face it at daybreak.

LA ATALAYA ✪✪

This once entirely troglodytic village 5km west of Santa Brígida (► 84) now has its fair share of free-standing buildings. But it continues to produce the kind of hand-made pottery first made by the aboriginal Canarios, without the use of the wheel and unglazed. It is sold by individual craftspeople from their cave workshops at the edge of the village. La Atalaya and the villages of Hoya de Pineda and Lugarejo are the main centres of pottery handicraft.

- 29E4
- ✉ Municipality of Santa Brígida: 12km south of Las Palmas, 52km north of Playa del Inglés
- 🚌 311 from Las Palmas
- 🔄 Caldera de Bandama (► 78)

LA GUANCHA ✪✪

On an arid site behind the sparkling sea, hemmed in by village houses and banana plantations, substantial remains of pre-Hispanic dwelling places and communal tombs survive. In the larger tombs, a central shaft is surrounded by two rows of radial chambers, all of it encircled by a final wall – like chapels lining the apse in a Christian cathedral. Forty-three people were buried in the largest.

- 28C6
- ✉ Municipality of Gáldar: 29km west of Las Palmas, 81km northwest of Playa del Inglés
- 🍴 Bar in El Agujero (€)
- 🎟 Free
- 🔄 Gáldar (► 80)

LOS BERRAZALES ✪✪

Set at the upper end of the Barranco de Agaete, Los Berrazales used to be a spa. An old-fashioned spa hotel, Princesa Guayarmina, still has guests but their activities are somewhat restricted now that the water is all bottled under the name Cumbres de Gáldar. Los Berrazales marks the start of the trail ascending inland to the high centre of the island and down to the north coast. Once it was busy with donkey traffic, grain moving one way and ground *gofio* the other. But the reservoirs above now retain all the water and the watermills are in ruins.

- 28C5
- ✉ Municipality of Agaete: 42km southwest of Las Palmas, 89km northwest of Playa del Inglés
- 🍴 Casa Romántica, Valle de Agaete (€€), Hotel Princesa Guayarmina (€€)
- 🚌 102 from Gáldar

Los Berrazales

🚹 29D5

✉️ Municipality of Moya: 34km southwest of Las Palmas, 87km north of Playa del Inglés

🍴 Los Tilos (€€€)

❓ On minor road off Moya-Guía road, 3km from Moya

LOS TILOS

The name refers to the surviving one per cent of Gran Canaria's original and ancient *laurasilva* (laurel) forest, still holding on here under rigorous protection. You may survey it from the very narrow road that runs through it but you are not allowed to wander in it. This is a tiny nature reserve, only about 200m long, made up of dense evergreen and varied species climbing up almost vertical banks from the stream bed.

🚹 29D5

✉️ Municipality of Moya: 31km west of Las Palmas, 90km north of Playa del Inglés

🍴 Cafés in town (€–€€€)

🚌 116, 117 from Las Palmas; 123 from Arucas

↔️ Los Tilos (► above)

Casa Museo Tomás Morales

✉️ Plaza de Tomás Morales 1

☎️ 928 62 02 17

🕐 Mon–Fri 9–8, Sat 10–8, Sun 10–2

🎟️ Free

Above: *the dramatically situated church at Moya*

MOYA

Seen from the west Moya is an astonishing place, with a huge church, Nuestra Señora de la Candelaria, perched on the very lip of a deep ravine. Small wonder that earlier churches on the same site collapsed into the *barranco*: the first in 1671, the next in 1704. A 15th-century image of the Virgin was preserved, however, and the town remains devoted to it. Moya has a delightful, lofty feel; the area set on the east side of the church, safely separated from the ravine, is well preserved. It includes the birthplace of the poet and doctor, Tomás Morales (1885–1921), at No 1 in the plaza now named after him – a fine, broad house with balcony, now the **Casa Museo Tomás Morales**. In prehistoric days, Moya was home town of the future leader Doramas, a poor boy who made good and moved to Telde when he became *guanarteme*, only to die resisting Spanish conquest. The town produces its own biscuits, *mimos* ('caresses') *de Moya* and *suspiros* ('sighs').

PUERTO DE LAS NIEVES ⭐⭐

Puerto de las Nieves is the home port of Agaete, capital in turn of a rich agricultural area. For centuries, this was the only reasonable point of access to this part of the island. A ferry service from Tenerife carries day-trippers and their hire cars in both directions. One dark grey beach huddles under the cliff, looking south at the Dedo de Dios (Finger of God), a slender monolith left standing when the rest of the cliff was eroded. Next comes the harbour and a promenade, the Paseo de las Poetas.

The 16th-century Ermita de la Virgen de las Nieves (Hermitage of the Virgin of the Snows) houses the central panel of the triptych of the *Virgin and Child* by the Flemish painter Joos van Cleve (1485–1540). The side panels, showing St Francis of Assisi and St Antony of Padua, are displayed in the church in Agaete (➤ 76). The panels are put together during the Bajada de la Rama fiesta, when the two villages get together to share the fun.

➕ 28B5
✉ Municipality of Agaete: 39km west of Las Palmas, 91km northwest of Playa del Inglés
🍴 Fish restaurants on Paseo de las Poetas (€–€€€)
🚌 103 from Las Palmas
⛴ Daily ferries to Tenerife (six ferries a day, 1-hour journey; www.fred.olsen.es)

Puerto de las Nieves, with the Finger of God in the foreground

The Argus Monitor from New Guinea, now at home in Reptilandia

REPTILANDIA ⚫⚫

Set on the dusty slopes of an extinct volcano (Montaña Almagro), this park breeds and displays reptiles and amphibians. Snakes from all over the world, many of them deadly, are housed in glass cases, all identified by scientific and common name (in English and in German) and place of origin. In addition to the three indoor exhibition rooms, there are large outoor terrariums of crocodiles, alligators, turtles, tortoises, lizards and frogs. These have been designed – with waist-high walls and a roof net – to allow the animals maximum protection in a natural-looking habitat which is also easily accessible to spectators. The owner is British zoologist Jim Pether. Don't miss the star attraction, the world's largest lizard, the Komodo dragon.

SANTA BRÍGIDA ⚫

This comfortable, bourgeois town is so well connected by fast road to Las Palmas, that it is now virtually a suburb of the capital city – and definitely well-heeled. Despite white-washed houses and Canarian balconies, Santa Brígida has less of a Spanish feel to it than any other town on the island. Its wide, tree-lined streets and large villas set in spacious gardens owe much to early British settlers, many of them involved in the wine, then the banana business. Though often working in the city, they made their homes here, attracted by the town's altitude and cooler temperatures. Santa Brígida and its neighbourhood are noted for their excellent restaurants (▶ 98).

28C5
Ctra Norte, km 24, Gáldar: 31km west of Las Palmas. From the south take GC1 to link with GC2 at Las Palmas, go on to Agaete, then follow signs from Hoya de Pineda exit
928 55 12 69
Daily 11–5:30
Snacks on premises (€)
102 to Cruz de Pineda, then follow signs for Reptilandia (1km)
Moderate

29D4
Municipality of Santa Brígida: 15km southwest of Las Palmas, 55km north of Playa del Inglés
301, 302, 303, 305 from Las Palmas
Caldera de Bandama (▶ 78)

SANTA MARÍA DE GUÍA ⭐⭐

Usually known simply as Guía, this town is situated 3km east of its neighbour and friendly rival, Gáldar. As in Gáldar, it pays to leave the main road and enter the old quarter, climbing briefly if steeply up narrow but stately streets (start where the road makes an awkward bend). The Las Palmas to Gáldar highway bypasses Guía and has restored the town to its early serenity.

Among the early settlers of Guía were Genoese bankers and merchants, so the town has the benefit of some fine architecture, such as the 16th-century Casa Quintana. As usual, the centrepiece is an old-fashioned main square with trees and a church (Santa María) in stern volcanic grey and white – in this case, however, with a floridly neo-classical façade designed by José Luján Pérez, Canarian sculptor–architect and native son of Guía. Begun in 1607, and mixing baroque with neo-classical, the interior of Santa María is colonial in feeling. The elegant town hall, in Canarian style, is also in the square. Guía is well known for craft – basketwork, carved-handled knives – but its most famous product is *queso de flor* ('flower-cheese'), made of goat's milk flavoured with artichoke flowers, best bought in the establishment belonging to Sr Santiago Giol, at Calle Marqués del Muni 34. This is a great barn of a shop, with cheeses laid out on bamboo mats, old photos of cheeses and cheese-makers, and wine bottles stacked all the way up the walls. There is no question of buying anything without first tasting it.

+ 28C5

✉ Municipality of Santa María de Guía: 24km west of Las Palmas, 76km northwest of Playa del Inglés

🍴 Cafés in town (€–€€€)

🚌 103, 105 from Las Palmas

↔ Cenobio de Valerón (► 19)

Below: *a parishioner at Guía's Santa María Church*

> ### Did you know ?
>
> The French composer, Camille Saint-Saëns, stayed and composed in Guía. Some of his works were first performed on the organ in the Church of Santa María

SARDINA

This is a little town of modern appearance right in the northwestern corner of the island. It faces south with views over the white-crested sea and along the coastline, with its magnificent cliffs. The town boasts some cave dwellings, cave boathouses and, as often, a cave restaurant. One is called, simply, La Cueva (➤ 99), tucked in where the road rounds the small but pleasing grey sand beach.

TAFIRA ALTA Y BAJA

Like their neighbour, Santa Brígida (➤ 84), the towns of Tafira Alta and Baja are now no more than comfortable residential suburbs of Las Palmas. They have large houses, ample gardens, and enjoy the proximity of the Jardín Canario (➤ 22) and the university campus. All is gracious suburban semi-rurality, spoiled only by the proximity of the busy 811 which runs through here from Las Palmas to Vega de San Mateo (➤ 90), passing through a narrow canyon of main street.

Light and shade on a wall in Tafira Baja, suburb of Las Palmas

Again like Santa Brígida, the area is known for good food (➤ 97–99). The Jardín Canario has an excellent restaurant and superb views by its top entrance. At the lower level, you can eat well in the village of La Calzada. The name of caves in the nearby barranco, Cuevas de los Frailes, recalls evangelising friars who were murdered by resistant Guanches. These same friars are immortalised in the name of a hotel, Los Frailes, built by an Englishman at the end of the 19th century, now a private house on the road above the Jardín Canario. Nearby Monte Lentiscal and Monte Coello are regarded as the best wine-producing area in the island.

TELDE ★★

Telde, in the east of the island and south of Las Palmas, is Gran Canaria's second largest town. Historically, it was the seat of the aboriginal king, or *guanarteme*, who controlled the eastern part of the island. Its environs are not inviting. Warehouses, factories and packing plants stretch down a dry and scrubby plain to the coastal motorway. The modern town centre is busy and thrumming with traffic. The old town centre, as anywhere on the island, is the best bit.

The most picturesque part is the *barrio* of San Francisco – a place of stone-coigned white houses, wooden balconies and pitched roofs around the 18th-century Church of San Francisco, home to rich merchants in earlier days. The major church, though, is San Juan Bautista (St John the Baptist), surrounded by cobbled streets and a pleasant square in the north of the town. It was begun early in the 16th century and finished in this century. Inside, above the ornate gilt *retablo*, is a life-sized figure of Christ sculpted from crushed maize, and weighing only some 5kg. It was made by Mexican Indians and indicates the amount of two-way traffic between the New World and the Canary Islands.

Telde is also the birthplace of the engineer who built the harbour at Las Palmas in 1882, Juan de León y Castillo. His former home is now a museum, the **Casa Museo León y Castillo**.

🕂 29E4

✉ Municipality of Telde: 21km south of Las Palmas, 77km northeast of Playa del Inglés

🚌 12 from Las Palmas; 36, 90 from Maspalomas

🔁 Cuatro Puertas (▶ 79)

Casa Museo León y Castillo

✉ Calle León y Castillo 43–45

☎ 928 69 13 77

🕐 Mon–Fri 9–8, Sat–Sun 10–1

🍴 Near museum (€–€€)

♿ Free

Above: *the bust of León y Castillo, the 19th-century engineer, outside his home, now a museum, in Telde*

🕂 29D5
✉ Municipality of Teror:
21km southwest of Las
Palmas, 77km north of
Playa del Inglés
🚌 216 from Las Palmas
🔄 Vega de San Mateo
(► 90)
❓ Town and island fiesta,
La Virgen del Pino, 8 Sep

**Casa Museo de los Patrones
de la Virgen**

✉ Plaza del Pino, 8
☎ 928 63 02 39
🕓 Mon–Thu and Sat 11–6,
Sun 10–2. Closed Fri
🍴 Near museum (€–€€)
💰 Moderate, free for
children under 10

Above: *a stone bench in
the quiet Plaza Teresa de
Bolívar, Teror*

TEROR ✪✪✪

Surrounded by green hills, the inland town of Teror is the island's greatest architectural gem, surviving unblemished in fine old Canarian style. One side of the imposing central square contains the basilica of Nuestra Señora de los Pinos, the Church of our Lady of the Pines, patron saint of the whole island. The other three sides of the square (and the complex of buildings behind the basilica), represent the best of manorial Canarian building.

The **Casa Museo de los Patrones de la Virgen** is a 17th-century mansion open as a museum when the owners are not in residence. Furnished rooms around a beautiful patio, particularly the domestic accommodation such as bedrooms and kitchen, are fascinating.

A small, irregularly shaped square leading off the Plaza del Pino is dedicated to Teresa de Bolívar, born in Teror. Her son was Simón Bolívar, the South American revolutionary hero. The country of Bolivia bears his name.

Time your visit for a Sunday morning, when a lively market for general and local goods takes place behind the church. Look out for specialities like marzipan cakes made by Cistercian nuns, varieties of bread, cheese and sausages – particularly the *chorizo rojo*, the red sausage of Teror (with a soft consistency, like a paste).

A Drive From Las Palmas

This drive sets off from the capital towards the mountainous centre of the island and returns through the agricultural village of Vega de San Mateo (➤ 90) and the prosperous villa town of Santa Brígida (➤ 84).

From Las Palmas pick up the GC300 at the city's edge through Tamaraceite. Follow signs for Teror and Arucas and at the road division, take the left GC21 to Teror.

This is the beginning of rurality. If you are exploring Teror, park behind the church.

Leave the town , and turn right after 1km on the Valleseco road, steadily climbing a road lined with eucalyptus. After 8km, you reach the look-out point, Mirador de Zamora.

High views look back over the town of Teror, and the large Restaurante Balcón Zamora does a brisk trade with coach parties.

After 2km, turn left to Artenara.

Soon you are up among pine woods, which give way to open hillsides of volcanic ash. Mirador de los Pinos de Gáldar offers views of the whole north coast, from the fishing village of Sardina (➤ 86) to Las Palmas.

From Artenara either continue to Tamadaba pine forest (another 7km) or leave on the road to Tejeda.

The Tejeda road follows the mountainside, with views to the west of Roque Bentaiga (➤ 69) and Roque Nublo (➤ 70).

Stop in Tejeda; return on GC110 to Cruz de Tejeda, centre point of the island (➤ 67). From Cruz de Tejeda, continue on the GC110 to Vega de San Mateo. Pass Santa Brígida and Tafira Alta to join the motorway into Las Palmas.

Distance
103 km

Time
About 6–7 hours with minimal stops

Start/end point
Las Palmas
✚ 29E5

Lunch
Restaurante Mirador Balcón de Zamora (€€)
✉ Carretera de Gran Canaria 21–13, Vallesco
☎ 928 61 80 42

89

PLAZA SAN JUAN
PLAZA MAYOR

🔲 29D4

✉ Municipality of Vega de
San Mateo: 21km
southwest of Las Palmas,
61km north of Playa del
Inglés

🚌 303 from Las Palmas

❓ Town fiesta, Romería de
San Mateo, 21 Sep

La Cantonera

✉ Avenida de Tinamar 17

☎ 928 66 17 95

🕐 Daily 10–3

🍴 Restaurant Mon–Sat 1–4,
9–midnight, Sun 1–4 (€€)

💷 Moderate

---

*Shopping for basketwork
in the Sunday morning
market at Vega de San
Mateo*

VEGA DE SAN MATEO ✪✪

Vega means 'fertile plain', and this prosperous town,
usually known as San Mateo, certainly deserves that
description – except in its hilliness. Almond, chestnut and
fig trees cover these foothills of the Tejeda crater. Well-
worked, terraced plots produce an abundance of fruit and
vegetables. The best pears and peaches on the island
come from San Mateo.

Traffic jams on the main street indicate the popularity of
San Mateo's Sunday morning market. However, only
farming stalwarts rise early enough to catch the livestock
market, held at first light. The general market takes place
in two huge hangars on the south side of town. One
contains stalls offering all the abundance of the land – fruit
and vegetables, bread, dried fruit, nuts and bunches of
sweet-smelling herbs, cakes and biscuits from Moya,
cheeses from San Nicolás. A second hangar is an
emporium of cassettes, old-fashioned felt slippers, jeans,
football scarves and sunglasses. In between the two,
traders lay their pottery and basketwork out on the ground.

The town's church, containing the 17th-century statue
of San Mateo, is fittingly dedicated to the patron saint of
farmers and cattle breeders. It was rebuilt in the last
century with the addition of a bell donated by Cuban
émigrés, former residents of San Mateo.

The **La Cantonera**, in a handsome, converted
farmhouse beside the main road, is a privately owned
museum of rural life, together with a 15-room hotel and an
excellent restaurant (➤ 98).

Where To...

Above: *poster advertising the local pub in Artenara*
Right: *Sioux City*

91

Las Palmas

Prices
Prices are approximate, based on a three-course meal for one without drinks and service:
€   = up to €12
€€ = €12–€24
€€€ = over €24

Acueducto (€€–€€€)
Initimate restaurant with wooden beams and an open grill. The place for carnivores, with an array of grilled meats.
✉ Sargento Llagas 45 ☎ 928 26 42 42 🕔 Lunch, dinner

Al-Andalus (€€)
Choose from a selection of tajines and other Morrocan dishes here, in what is claimed to be the only Arabic restaurant on the island.
✉ C/Tomás Miller ☎ 928 22 22 01 🕔 Fri, Sat and festivals 12–4, 8–midnight, Sun 12–4. Phone for other days

Amaiur (€€€)
One of the best eating places in the city specilises in the delicious subtly spicey tastes of Basque cuisine.
✉ C/Pérez Galdós 2 ☎ 928 37 07 17 🕔 Mon–Sat 1–4 8:30–12

Café Madrid (€)
In one of the loveliest squares in the city, this is a good place for a drink or the excellent value menu of the day.
✉ Plaza de Cairasco 2 ☎ 928 36 06 64 🕔 Lunch, dinner

Ca'Cho Damian (€€)
If you're shopping in the Ballena Mall, stop here for tasty *tapas* or a good meal of traditional Canarian fare.
✉ CC La Ballena ☎ 928 41 73 00 🕔 All day

Café de la Vegueta (€)
The popular evening bar-restaurant has good *tapas* and imaginative dishes of the day based on what's best from the nearby market.
✉ C/Mendizábal 24 ☎ 928 33 13 21 🕔 Tue–Sun 4PM–2:30AM

Canguro (€)
For the biggest croissants and cakes around, try this snack bar. A good place for breakfast before looking around Vegueta market.
✉ C/Calvo Sotelo 1 ☎ 928 33 02 55 🕔 Open normal shopping hours

Casa Carmelo (€€€)
Excellent grilled meat and fish of your choice. Friendly atmosphere.
✉ Paseo de las Canteras 2 ☎ 928 46 90 56 🕔 Lunch, dinner

Casa Montesdeoca (€€€)
An elegant dining room and patio restaurant set in a restored mansion with an attractive courtyard. Noted for its fish dishes.
✉ C/Montesdeoca 10 ☎ 928 33 34 66 🕔 Lunch, dinner. Closed Sun

Don Quijote (€€)
Don't expect Spanish food in this restaurant. The flavour here is international, specifically Belgian, with the emphasis on steak.
✉ C/Secretario Artiles 74 ☎ 928 27 27 86 🕔 Lunch, dinner

El Cerdo Que Rie (€)
Mostly grills. Moderate prices for good food, especially flambés and fondues.
✉ Paseo de las Canteras 31 ☎ 928 26 36 49 🕔 Lunch, dinner

El Corte Ingles (€€€)
The popular lunchtime restaurant in this prestigious department store serves excellent food from an international menu.
✉ Avda Mesa y Lopez 18

WHERE TO EAT & DRINK

☎ 928 26 20 00 🕐 Lunch.
Closed Sun and hols

El Herreño (€–€€)
A pleasant rustic feel to this
excellent restaurant whose
owner comes from El Hierro,
one of the Canary Islands.
The menu reflects traditional
Canarian cooking; try the
delicious roast pork.
☎ C/Mendizábal 5 ☎ 928 31
05 13 🕐 9AM–1AM

El Novillo Precoz (€€€)
A popular, family-run steak
restaurant. Beef is flown in
from Uruguay three times a
week.
☎ C/Portugal 9 ☎ 928 22 16 59
🕐 Lunch, dinner. Closed Mon

El Padrino (€€)
Above the Puerto de la Luz
in Las Coloradas, this popular
restaurant serves excellent
fish and seafood and typical
Canarian dishes.
☎ C/Jesús Nazareno 1 ☎ 928
46 85 72 🕐 Lunch, dinner

El Pote (€€€)
Galician food and wine is the
speciality here, although
Canarian dishes like potatoes
in mojo sauce and rabbit
stew are excellent.
☎ Pasaje Juan Manuel Durán
41 ☎ 928 27 80 58 🕐 Lunch,
dinner. Sun lunch only

Hipócrates (€€)
Close to the Casa de Colón
in the old part of the city, this
restaurant serves fresh,
delectable salads and
vegetarian food.
☎ C/Colón 4 ☎ 928 31 11 71
🕐 Lunch, dinner

Julio (€€€)
A restaurant decorated in
nautical style; naturally, offers
fish and seafood as its
speciality. The chef produces
excellent roast and grilled
meat, too, and Canarian
dishes served with a selection
of wine from all the islands.
☎ C/La Naval 132 ☎ 928 46 01
39 🕐 Lunch, dinner. Closed Sun

La Casita (€€€)
On the edge of Parque
Doramas, this restaurant, in
two dining rooms and a
covered terrace, caters for
the discerning bourgeoisie.
Extensive wine list.
☎ C/León y Castillo 227
☎ 928 24 54 64 🕐 Lunch,
dinner

La Marinera (€€–€€€)
Wonderful panoramic views
of the bay from this
restaurant that serves grills –
barbeque style – with meats
from Uruguay and Argentina.
Good fish, too.
☎ Paseo de las Canteras 2
C/Alonso Ojeda ☎ 928 46 88 02
🕐 12:30–midnight

La Pasta Real (€€)
Italian cooking, excellent
pasta and good variety of
vegetarian dishes.
☎ C/Secretario Padilla 28
☎ 928 26 22 67
🕐 Lunch, dinner. Closed Tue

Meson Condado (€€)
An unpretentious, friendly
restaurant with fish and
seafood cooked in the
Galician manner.
☎ C/Ferreras 22 ☎ 928 46 94
43 🕐 Lunch, dinner

Rías Bajas (€€€)
A popular but pricey
restaurant serving fish and
seafood in Galician style with
excellent wine from
northwest Spain.
☎ C/Simón Bolívar 3 ☎ 928
27 13 16 🕐 Lunch, dinner

Wine
Wine is now produced in
only one small area of the
island – El Monte – about
10km south of Las
Palmas. There have been
efforts made recently to
improve the quality of the
wine, but most people
agree that its charm lies in
its rough-and-ready
country taste.

The South

Fresh Fish
Most visitors are familiar with the Spanish dish *paella* – a mixture of flavoured rice and seafood – but it is not an island speciality. Fish restaurants here pride themselves on really fresh fish: try it grilled or baked.

Faro 2 Shopping Centre
This vast centre in Maspalomas has a large number of restaurants, cafés and bars with food ranging from traditional Canarian to Italian and Mexican. Plenty of choice for all the family.

Agüimes
La Tartería (€)
Located in the old square, close to the church of St Sebastián, this is a nice place for a snack with good homemade cakes and pies. Good choice of coffees and ice creams. Nice welcome and friendly service.

✉ Plaza del Rosario 21
☎ 928 78 77 38 ⏰ Lunch, dinner

Tagoror (€€)
Praised as much for its location – high above the Guayadeque ravine – as for its food: strictly the best of Canarian. The Tagoror is an essential restaurant.

✉ Montaña Las Tierras, 21, Guayadeque ☎ 928 17 20 13
⏰ Lunch, dinner

Arguineguín
Bahía (€€)
Overlooking the harbour in this pretty resort, this friendly restaurant serves tourists and locals alike with excellent fresh fish dishes at reasonable prices.

✉ Avenida. Del Muelle 6
☎ 928 73 53 81
⏰ 10:30AM–10:30PM

Bar Cofradía de Pescadores (€€)
This fishermen's co-operative serves fresh fish straight off the fishing boats in the harbour. A simple, neighbourhood restaurant with a far-reaching reputation among both locals and visitors. The blackboard menu also offers alternatives for meat-eaters. Seating inside and out. At the very end of the harbour.

✉ Avenida del Muelle s/n
☎ 928 73 59 56 ⏰ Lunch, dinner. Closed Mon

Maspalomas/Playa del Inglés/San Agustin
Amaiur (€€€)
This top restaurant serves superb food from the Spanish Basque region. Try the *lomo de merluza con almejas* – hake in clam sauce.

✉ Avenida Neckerman, Maspalomas 42 ☎ 928 76 44 14
⏰ Lunch, dinner. Closed Sun

Boccalino (€–€€)
On the beach, this snack-bar/restaurant is cheerful and inviting with its bright tablecloths, yellow paintwork, tiled walls and wooden beams. Try the paella or the fresh fish.

✉ Playa de Las Barras, San Agustín ☎ 928 76 60 18
⏰ Lunch, dinner. Closed Sun

Chipi-Chipi (€€)
Courteous service and good food, well presented at moderate cost, is the hallmark of this unpretentious little restaurant.

✉ Avenida Tirajana, Ed Barbados 1, Playa del Inglés ☎ 928 76 50 88 ⏰ Lunch, dinner

El Duomo di Milano (€€)
This restaurant serves some excellent Italian and Mediterranean dishes.

✉ C/Hannover 4, Playa del Inglés ☎ 928 76 37 95
⏰ 12–4, 7–12

El Portalón (€€€)
An elegant restaurant, as successful in meat as in fish cookery with a good wine list.

✉ Avenida Tirajana 27, Playa del Inglés ☎ 928 77 16 22
⏰ Lunch, dinner

Gorbea (€€€)

The restaurant of the Hotel Gloria Palace is open to non-residents for dinner. It offers stunning views from the ninth floor and excellent Basque cuisine with an emphasis on fish and seafood.

✉ **Las Margaritas, San Agustín**
☎ **928 76 83 00**
🕐 **Dinner. Closed Sun & Jun**

Guatiboa (€€€)

A top Canarian restaurant, part of a top hotel – the IFA Faro Maspalomas, just yards away from the beach – serves excellent food in sumptuous surroundings.

✉ **Plaza de Faro 1, Maspalomas** ☎ **928 14 22 14**
🕐 **Dinner**

La Casa Vieja (€–€€)

This is, in fact, two restaurants on either side of the road. On the left as you come up the hill is the more traditional, serving chargrilled meats. On the right, El Rincón, the more expensive option, specialises in fish. Book ahead for a table in the garden.

✉ **El Lomo, Carrtera a Fataga**
☎ **928 76 99 18** 🕐 **Lunch, dinner**

La Foresta (€€–€€€)

Poolside restaurant of the Riu Grand Palace hotel in Maspalomas that serves a good-value buffet lunch. The main menu is expensive but you can opt for salads and desserts. Lovely gardens.

✉ **Hotel Riu Grand Palace Maspalomas Oasis, Playa de Maspalomas** ☎ **928 14 14 48**
🕐 **Lunch only**

La Toja (€€€)

Excellent fish restaurant in two dining rooms in the centre of Playa del Inglés. *Caldo de pescado*, fish and vegetable soup, is delicious.

✉ **Avenida Tirajana 17, Playa del Inglés** ☎ **928 76 11 96**
🕐 **Lunch, dinner. Closed Sun**

Las Cumbres Canarias(€€)

Typically Spanish restaurant serves excellent roast lamb.

✉ **Avenida de Tirajana 9, Playa del Inglés** ☎ **928 76 09 41** 🕐 **Lunch, dinner**

Loopy's (€€)

Grilled meat and pizzas and a lively atmosphere in a Swiss-chalet-type restaurant.

✉ **Las Retamas 7, San Agustín**
☎ **928 76 28 92**
🕐 **Lunch, dinner**

Los Pescadores (€)

It is only due to the high level of tourism that this restaurant includes pizzas on its menu. Well-known for its typically Canarian dishes this one serves mainly fish, plus a good selection of grilled meats.

✉ **Bahía Feliz, San Agustín**
☎ **928 15 71 79** 🕐 **Lunch, dinner**

Marieta Buffet Grill (€–€€)

One of many self-service restaurants – good value, huge selections, you can eat all you want. They do breakfast, too.

✉ **Avenida Italia 15, Playa del Inglés** ☎ **928 77 34 14**
🕐 **Lunch, dinner**

Mogán

Grill Acaymo (€€)

Rustic décor combined with thrilling terrace views. Canarian food a speciality here.

✉ **El Tostador 14**
☎ **928 56 92 63**
🕐 **12–10.30. Closed Sun evening and Mon**

Sancocho

Sancocho is a favourite traditional meal on the island. It is the sort of meal served to the whole family for Sunday lunch, causing much smacking of lips and kissing of fingers – but it may be an acquired taste. It is a dish of salt *cherne*, like bass (the saltier the better), served with boiled potatoes and *gofio*, either as dumplings or to thicken the gravy.

Meat Eaters

Canarians are great meat eaters; beef (*carne de vacca*), usually of excellent quality, is flown in from South America. Pork (*cerdo*), lamb (*cordero*) and kid (*cabrito*) are local products. So, too, is rabbit (*conejo*), most typically eaten as *conejo en salmorejo* – rabbit cooked in onion, red pepper and oregano, and served in a piquant sauce.

Puerto Mogán

El Faro (€€)

A great location in a small 'lighthouse' at the end of the fishing harbour. You can sip a drink or attack a grilled fish while looking at the view.

✉ Puerto de Mogán ☎ 928 56 52 85 🕐 Lunch, dinner

La Bodeguilla Juananá (€€)

Bar-restaurant plus deli serving and selling local food and handicrafts.

✉ Puerto de Mogán ☎ 928 56 50 44 🕐 Dinner only

La Cofradía de Pescadores (€€)

Popular with locals and tourists, this fishermen's cooperative by the harbour produces good fresh grilled fish. Try the warm bread with garlic mayonnaise.

✉ Dársena Exterior del Puerto ☎ 928 56 53 21 🕐 Lunch, dinner

Patio Canario II (€€–€€€)

Specialising in fish, this attractive restaurant also serves grills and Canarian fare.

✉ Puerto de Mogán ☎ 928 56 52 74 🕐 Lunch, dinner

Tu Casa (€€)

Fish is the speciality here. Try the *parrillada de pescado* – variety of grilled fish.

✉ Avenida de las Artes 18 ☎ 928 56 50 78 🕐 Lunch, dinner. Closed Tue

Puerto Rico

Don Quijote (€€)

International cuisine at low prices. Children's menu.

✉ Centro Comercial ☎ 928 56 09 01 🕐 Lunch, dinner. Closed Sun

El Tiburón (€€)

Translated as 'the shark', this restaurant offers different types of fresh fish as well as some excellent pizzas. You may be lured in with offers of free *sangria*.

✉ Paseo Maritimo ☎ 928 56 05 57 🕐 Lunch, dinner

Gran Canaria (€€)

Not just barbecued meat and fish by the beach here. This restaurant has huge steaks, great desserts – complete with flaming sparklers – and live music.

✉ Playa de Puerto Rico ☎ 928 56 13 54 🕐 Lunch, dinner

La Cantina (€€–€€€)

Although mainly renonwned for its wines and aperitifs, you can get a good steak or have a fondue. Don't miss a look at the impressive wine cellar.

✉ Apartmentos El Greco, Calle Doreste y Molina ☎ 928 56 00 40 🕐 Lunch, dinner

Central Gran Canaria & the North

Agaete

Casa Pepe (€€)
A cheerful, popular place to eat meat or fish. Good value.
- ✉ C/Alcalde Armas Galván 5
- ☎ 928 89 82 27
- ⏱ Lunch, dinner. Closed Wed

Casa Romántica (€€)
A delightful restaurant which serves both international and Spanish food using fresh produce.
- ✉ Valle de Agaete, km 3.5
- ☎ 928 89 80 84
- ⏱ Lunch only

Princesa Guayarmina (€€€)
The restaurant of a former spa hotel, a little run-down but sweetly old-fashioned, serves Canarian food surrounded by splendid scenery.
- ✉ Valle de Agaete, km 7
- ☎ 928 89 80 09
- ⏱ Lunch, dinner

Artenara
There are some *tapas* bars and inexpensive eating places on Avenida Matías Vega.

Arucas

Casa Brito (€–€€)
This smart restaurant with rustic decoration opened in 1998. Good choice of Canarian and Argentinian dishes, including *morcilla canaria* (Canarian black pudding). Small wine list.
- ✉ Pasaje de Ter 17
- ☎ 928 62 23 23
- ⏱ Lunch, dinner. Closed Mon and Tue

El Mesón de la Montaña (€€–€€€)
With exceptional views of the Montaña de Arucas – a rather touristy spot – this restaurant has a versatile cuisine ranging from traditional Canarian to other European fare. Try the *calabacines rellenos de gambas* (stuffed courgettes with prawns). Good wine list.
- ✉ Montaña de Arucas
- ☎ 928 60 08 44
- ⏱ Lunch, dinner

La Barca (€€)
Much praised fish and seafood restaurant in San Andrés, a fishing hamlet in the municipality of Arucas. Your choice depends on the day's catch.
- ✉ Carretera del Norte 26, San Andrés
- ☎ 928 62 60 88
- ⏱ Lunch, dinner. Closed Mon

Firgas

Asaderos Las Brasas (€)
Well known for its chickens, roasted in charcoal grills, this is a typical informal country restaurant, popular with locals as well as tourists. Good value.
- ✉ Avenida de La Cruz 36
- ☎ 928 62 52 50
- ⏱ Lunch, dinner. Closed Tue

Gáldar

Alcori Restaurante (€€)
Cheerful, bustling, town-centre restaurant.
- ✉ C/ Capitán Quesada
- ☎ 928 88 27 12
- ⏱ Lunch, dinner

La Atalaya

El Castillete (€€)
Select and cook your own meat at the barbecue or on a hot stone at your table. Very popular restaurant, so reserve ahead at weekends.
- ✉ El Raso 7, La Atalya
- ☎ 928 35 24 43
- ⏱ Closed dinner Sun and Mon

Fish
Even on an island, demand for fish (*pescado*) can often outstrip supply. Beware of thawed frozen fish sold as fresh. Good, fresh fish is expensive, even if it is bought straight out of the fisherman's nets. Tuna, cod, hake, swordfish, mackerel and sardines are familiar to everyone and are available on most menus. Try the local varieties like *cherne* (similar to bass), *sama* (like sea bream) and, a speciality in Gran Canaria, *vieja* (like parrotfish).

Canarian Beer
Most Canarios drink beer, *cerveza*, with their food. A small glass of beer is a *caña*. *Tropical* is the major island brand, but *Dorada* from Tenerife is also popular. All international brands are available on the island.

Puerto de las Nieves

Capita (€€)
Freshest fish, in this friendly, bustling, cheerful restaurant.
✉ Puerto de las Nieves 37
☎ 928 55 41 42
🕐 Lunch, dinner

El Dedo de Dios (€€€)
Seafood soup and fish stew with *gofio* is the speciality here – Canarian fish cooking at its best.
✉ Puerto de las Nieves
☎ 928 89 80 00
🕐 Lunch, dinner

El Puerto de Laguete (€€)
Crowded at weekends and never empty during the week, this fish restaurant is famous for its food and its atmosphere.
✉ Nuestra Señora de las Nieves 9 ☎ 928 55 40 01
🕐 Lunch, dinner. Closed Mon

Faneque (€€€)
This smart restaurant in the Hotel Puerto de las Nieves offers high-quality international and Canarian cooking, using both meat and fish.
✉ Carretera Anton Cerezo
☎ 928 88 62 56
🕐 Lunch, dinner. Closed Sun

Las Nasas (€€€)
A superb fish restaurant in an area renowned for fish eateries. Terrace to the beach.
✉ C/Puerto de las Nieves 6, Agaete ☎ 928 89 86 50
🕐 Lunch, dinner

Santa Brígida

Bentayga (€€)
First-class restaurant using the best of local produce in local cuisine. The meat dishes – try lamb or goat – are highly recommended.
✉ Carretera del Centro 130, Monte Coello
☎ 928 35 51 86
🕐 8:30AM–1AM

Casa Martel (€€€)
Old-fashioned country restaurant with an excellent wine cellar.
✉ Carretera del Centro, km 18, El Madroñal ☎ 928 64 24 83
🕐 Lunch, dinner

Grutas de Artiles (€€€)
Reputation for serving good Spanish food in a lively setting that includes a garden, tennis courts, swimming pool and caves.
✉ Las Meleguiñas, Santa Brígida ☎ 928 64 05 75; www.lasgrutasdeartiles.com
🕐 Noon–12:30AM

Los Geranios (€)
Famous for roast and grilled pork and local red wine, this simple village bar is crowded at weekends.
✉ Barrio de Bandama
☎ None 🕐 Lunch, dinner

Pizzería California (€€)
Tasty pizzas, light meals and sandwiches in a cheerful neighbourhood café.
✉ C/Manuel Hernández Muñoz 5 ☎ 928 64 27 03
🕐 Lunch, dinner

Satautey (€€)
This restaurant in the Hotel Escuela (a working hotel and a hotel training school) wins enthusiastic plaudits for the quality of food and service – a testimony to the professionalism of the catering students in charge.
✉ C/Real de Coello 2, Santa Brígida ☎ 828 01 04 21
🕐 1:30–4, 7:30–11

Santa Lucía

Hao (€€)
Country food is served at this mountainside village. The restaurant is particularly popular with visitors to the neighbouring Museum of Canarian Life. Arrive before 12:30, or after 2, to avoid coach parties.
✉ C/Tomas Arroyo Cardosa
☎ 928 79 80 07 🕐 Lunch

San Mateo

La Cantonera (€€)
Good country cooking in an old farmhouse which has been turned into a museum of rural life and an excellent hotel in lovely surroundings.

✉ Avenida Tinamar ☎ 928 33 13 74 🕐 Lunch. Closed Sun

La Veguetilla (€€€)
This is an ideal restaurant in which to enjoy a long, slow Sunday lunch. Canarian and Spanish food, beautifully cooked and served.

✉ Carretera del Centro km 20.300 ☎ 928 66 07 64
🕐 Lunch, dinner. Closed Tue

Sardina

La Cueva (€€)
A small cave restaurant serving fresh fish, either in the cave or on the terrace outside. Simple but sweet.

✉ Playa de Sardina ☎ 928 88 02 36 🕐 Lunch, dinner

Miguelín (€€)
A simple fish restaurant. Each dish is freshly prepared and cooked to order. Excellent value.

✉ Carretera de Sardina, km 5, 79 ☎ 928 88 00 15
🕐 Lunch, dinner. Closed Mon

Tafira

Jardín Canario (€€€)
A wonderful setting on the edge of the cliff above the botanical gardens. The food is excellent Canarian, the service is elegant.

✉ Carretera del Centro, km 7.200, Tafira Alta
☎ 928 43 09 39
🕐 Lunch, dinner

La Masia de Canarias (€€€)
Country restaurant serving wholesome Canarian food from fresh local ingredients.

✉ C/ Murillo 36, Tafira Alta
☎ 928 35 01 20
🕐 Lunch, dinner

Tejeda

Cueva de la Tea (€€)
A good, unpretentious restaurant in Tejeda, specialising in roast meat.

✉ C/Dr Hernández Guerra
🕐 Lunch

El Refugio (€€)
In an incomparable situation among the high peaks of the island, this restaurant, popular with coach parties, offers a Canarian menu that is both filling and delicious.

✉ Cruz de Tejeda
☎ 928 66 65 13;
www.hotelruralrefugio.com
🕐 Lunch

Yolanda (€€–€€€)
Next door to El Refugio, with wonderful views from the balcony (across to Tenerife weather permitting). Excellent hearty mountain fare of roast meats served with local vegetables, plus some international dishes.

✉ Cruz de Tejeda
☎ 928 66 62 76 🕐 Daily 9-7

Telde

La Pardilla (€€)
Northeast of Telde, this restaurant is highly praised for its traditional Canarian cuisine, particularly its *mojo* sauces to accompany charcoal-grilled meat. The *puchero canario*, a rich meat and vegetable stew, is another favourite.

✉ C/Raimundo Lulio 54, La Pardilla ☎ 928 69 51 02
🕐 Lunch, dinner. Closed Mon

Teror

Balcón de la Zamora (€€)
Fine views from the look-out point and excellent kid stew in this busy restaurant.

✉ Carretera a Vallesseco km 8
☎ 928 61 80 42
🕐 Lunch, dinner

Vegetarians
Vegetarians may feel sadly neglected in island restaurants despite the quality and variety of local vegetables. A meal consisting only of vegetables is a novel concept to most Canarian cooks, who will happily produce a vegetable stew full of beans, carrots, sweet potatoes and artichokes, then add a blood sausage or pork chop for supposed extra nutrition. Similarly, when you order a salad, it is worth mentioning if you do not want tuna (*atun*) or egg (*huevo*) added.

Las Palmas

Prices

Prices are for a double room, excluding breakfast and VAT.

€ = up to €60
€€ = €60–€120
€€€ = over €120

The rates vary enormously, depending on the season and the state of the local economy.

Capital Hotels

Although early tourists preferred the north of the island and made their base in Las Palmas, the choice of hotel accommodation in the capital is now rather limited in comparison with what is on offer in the southern resorts. In general, visitors who choose to stay in Las Palmas tend to be business travellers or those in flight from other tourists.

Astoria (€€)

A modern hotel near Playa de las Canteras with terrace, swimming pool, gym and squash courts.

✉ C/Fernándo Guanarteme 54
☎ 928 22 27 50

Atlanta (€€)

Good facilities in this friendly hotel, only a few minutes from the beach. There are 64 rooms and 7 suites all with air-conditioning.

✉ C/Alfredo L Jones 37
☎ 928 27 80 00;
www.atlantacanarias.com

Cantur (€€)

Comfortable, 1960s-built hotel with terrace; many rooms with view of Playa de las Canteras. Breakfast included. 124 rooms.

✉ C/Sagasta 26 ☎ 928 27 33 78; www.hotelcantur.com

Colón (€€)

An apartment block situated at the beach end of this busy street. Go for the sea-view rooms. 38 rooms.

✉ C/Alfredo Jones 45
☎ 928 22 08 76

Concorde (€€€)

A modern hotel with 124 rooms, comfortable and well-run, close to Canteras beach and Parque Santa Catalina. Swimming pool.

✉ C/Tomás Miller 85
☎ 928 26 27 50;
www.hotelconcorde.org

Fataga (€€)

A middle-range hotel in the business area of the city within easy walking distance of both Canteras and Alcaravaneras beaches. 92 rooms.

✉ C/Nestor de la Torre 21
☎ 928 29 06 14

Faycan (€)

Moderately priced, clean and comfortable hotel with 61 rooms in a central situation.

✉ C/Nicolas Estevanez 61
☎ 928 27 06 54

Hotel AC Gran Canaria (€€)

The circular tower of this hotel, equally accessible from Canteras Beach and the Parque Santa Catalina, dominates the city skyline. Formerly luxurious but now in need of renovation work, it offers glorious views. 227 rooms, solarium and swimming pool

✉ C/Eduardo Benot 3
☎ 928 26 61 00;
www.ac-hotels.com

Hotel Idafe (€)

Basic but clean, this hotel with 34 rooms is centrally located, not far from the beach.

✉ C/Nicolas Estevanez 49
☎ 928 26 56 74

Hotel Igramar Canteras (€€)

Only 50m from the beach this hotel with 61 rooms is clean and comfortable and also offers access for visitors with disabilities.

✉ C/Columbia 12
☎ 928 47 29 60

Hotel Madrid (€)

Built in 1910, and favoured by artists and intellectuals (General Franco stayed in room 3 in 1936) this friendly family-run hotel is slowly being updated.

✉ Plaza de Cairasco 2
☎ 928 36 06 64

Hotel Parque (€€)

Well situated for the old town, just across the road from the Parque San Telmo, this is an excellent middle-range hotel. Good bus service to southern resorts from nearby bus station. 102 rooms.

✉ **Muelle de las Palmas** ☎ 928 36 80 00; www.hparque.com

Hotel Pujol (€)
A good budget hotel with 48 rooms and easy access to the port and Canteras Beach.

✉ **C/Salvador Cuyas 5**
☎ 928 27 94 89

Hotel Residencia Majórica (€)
Right on Parque Santa Catalina and therefore likely to be noisy, this hotel is nevertheless clean and cheap.

✉ **C/Ripoche 22** ☎ 928 26 28 78

Hotel Tryp Iberia (€€)
Very comfortable hotel in a good location right on the promenade with panoramic views to the sea. Facilities include a beauty centre, swimming pool and 297 rooms all with shower.

✉ **Avda Alcalde José Ramírez Bethencourt 8** ☎ 928 36 11 33

Imperial Playa (€€€)
Pleasant, comfortable hotel on the north end of Canteras beach, complete with satellite TV and air-conditioning. Excellent breakfast. Sauna and squash courts. 142 rooms.

✉ **C/Ferreras 1** ☎ 928 46 88 54

Marsin Playa (€€)
Comfortable apartments facing the beach at Las Canteras. It is worth paying the extra to get the sea views.

✉ **C/Luis Morote 54**
☎ 928 27 08 08

Meliá Las Palmas (€€€)
Luxury hotel in the middle of Playa de las Canteras, with 312 rooms, shops, disco and a swimming pool.

✉ **C/Gomera 6** ☎ 928 26 80 50

Reina Isabel (€€€)
Luxury hotel in an unrivalled position on the Canteras Beach, with a superb high-rise restaurant, Parrilla Reina Isabel, and a gym and swimming pool on the roof terrace. 231 rooms.

✉ **C/Alfredo L Jones 40**
☎ 928 26 01 00

Sansofé Palace (€€€)
An excellent modern hotel, it occupies a fine position, near Canteras Beach. 115 rooms.

✉ **C/Portugal 68**
☎ 928 22 40 62

Santa Catalina (€€€)
Gran Canaria's top city hotel in a quiet, shady park. Canarian architecture, fine restaurant – Restaurante Doramas – and a casino. Tennis and squash courts, swimming pool. 208 rooms.

✉ **León y Castillo 227, Parque Doramas** ☎ 928 24 30 40

Tenesoya (€€–€€€)
This is more a business than a tourist hotel, with straightforward unpretentious comforts and no restaurant. But facilities are of a good standard, service is friendly and efficient, and it is very close to Canteras Beach. There are 43 rooms.

✉ **C/Sagasta 98**
☎ 928 46 96 08

Verol (€–€€)
Good value hotel with 25 rooms located only one minute from the beach. The café/bar is popular.

✉ **C/Sagasta 25**
☎ 928 26 21 04

La Guagua Turística
The Las Palmas tourist bus is a great way to see the city. This open-top bus service operates daily from 9:30AM until 5:45PM. Tickets are valid for the whole day and are very reasonably priced. You can get on and off at any stop throughout the day. Commentary is in English, Spanish and German. Tickets are available from the bus station at Parque San Telmo and on the bus itself. The two-hour circuit of the city begins and ends at Parque Santa Catalina.

Lateen Sailing
Lateen sailing is a sport peculiar to this island. Small boats with huge sails race around the Bay of Las Palmas between April and September. Watch them (Saturday afternoon and Sunday morning) from the Avenida Marítima in Las Palmas.

The South

For Tennis Fans

Tennis players – or would-be tennis players – in search of total immersion in the game should book into the Helga Masthoff Park & Sport Hotel (€€€) closed June. ✉ Barranco de los Palmitos (☎ 928 14 21 00) for six artificial grass courts, swimming pool, sauna and a sporty atmosphere. Not far from here, in Monte Leon, is an exclusive and well-hidden millionaire's enclave of sumptuous villas, the haunt of international celebrities (mostly musicians) and heads of state. No hotels, though.

Arguineguín
Anfi del Mar (€€)

Luxury aparthotel with every comfort, swimming pools, restaurants, tropical gardens, marina and a beach of white Caribbean sand. Exceptional value.

✉ Barranco de la Verga
☎ 928 15 00 59; www.anfi.com

Maspalomas/Playa del Inglés/San Agustín
Gloria Palace (€€)

Large, well-established hotel in San Augustín with a new thalassotherapy (sea-water therapy) centre (☎ 928 77 64 04) adjacent which is open to non-residents.

✉ Las Margaritas, San Augustín ☎ 928 12 85 00

Grand Hotel Residencia (€€€)

This designer hotel, opened in 2000, is fast becoming one of the most exclusive on the island, with attractive rooms in villas set around a pool.

✉ Avda del Oasis 32, Maspalomas ☎ 928 72 31 00

H10 Playa Meloneras Palace (€€€)

Just west of Maspalomas this luxury hotel with 351 rooms is beautifully set above the beach. Choice of restaurants and bars; two swimming pools, sports centre. Elegance with traditional Canarian style.

✉ Carretera Mar Caspio, Playa Meloneras, Maspalomas
☎ 928 12 82 82

IFA Faro Maspalomas (€€€)

Luxury hotel metres away from the lighthouse after which it is named. The sea views are glorious, the hotel restaurant Guatiboa (➤ 95) is one of the best on the island and guests are entitled to a discount on the Maspalomas golf course green fees.

✉ Plaza del Faro, Maspalomas
☎ 928 14 29 91

Meliá Tamarindos (€€€€)

Luxury hotel in a quiet situation with superb gardens; casino and cabaret on premises.

✉ Las Retamas 3, San Agustín
☎ 928 77 40 90

Palacio Dunamar (€€€)

An incomparable position on the beach and the views from sea-facing rooms make this hotel special. Swimming pool, squash.

✉ Avenida de Helsinki 8, Playa del Inglés ☎ 928 76 50 11

Riu Grand Palace Maspalomas Oasis (€€€)

Undoubtedly the most luxurious hotel in the south, the Oasis is situated on the beach, beside the dunes and surrounded by palms.

✉ Plaza de las Palmeras Playa de Maspalomas
☎ 928 14 14 48; www.riu.com

Riu Palace Meloneras (€€€)

A grand, white wedding-cake of a hotel, with apartment chalets on lawns around a pool. The complex includes a golf course, conference centre and shopping mall.

✉ Urbanización Las Meloneras ☎ 928 14 31 82

Puerto Mogán
Hotel Taurito Princess (€€€)

A splendid hotel above the beach just outside Puerto Mogán. Great views of garden, pool and coast.

✉ Playa de Taurito, Mogán
☎ 928 56 53 10

Central Gran Canaria & the North

Agaete

Hotel Princesa Guayarmina (€€)

An old-fashioned spa hotel in a green and fertile valley. Ideal for quiet walks.

✉ **Los Berrazales, Valle de Agaete** ☎ **928 89 80 09**

La Casa Roja (€€–€€€)

In a beautiful situation, this 19th-century mansion was recently renovated into a country hotel.

✉ **C/Doctor Chil 20, Valle de Agaete km 4** ☎ **928 89 81 45**

Agüimes

Casa de los Camellos (€€)

Lovely rural hotel renovated from a 300-year-old stone barn set around courtyards and gardens. 12 rooms.

✉ **C/Progreso 12** ☎ **928 78 50 03**

Arucas

La Hacienda del Buen Suceso (€€€)

High-quality rural hotel overlooking banana plantations with views to the sea. Pool, Jacuzzi and fitness room.

✉ **Carretera de Arucas a Bañaderos, km 1** ☎ **928 62 29 45**

Fataga

Molino del Agua (€€)

A small, rural hotel in the Fataga valley with offers of camel rides, hearty Canarian cooking. Swimming pool.

✉ **Carretera Fataga a San Bartolome km 1** ☎ **928 17 20 89**

Puerto de las Nieves

Hotel Puerto de las Nieves (€€€)

Luxury hotel with many facilities including sauna, Jacuzzi and therapy treatments. Close to beach.

✉ **C/ Anton Cerezo** ☎ **928 88 62 56**

San Mateo

Hotel Rural el Pinar (€€€)

Nine beautifully furnished, rustic rooms. Off the road between Valsequillo and San Mateo, this is an ideal place to walk or relax by the pool. Evening meal by request.

✉ **La Parada 26 (Tenteniguada), Valsequillo** ☎ **928 70 52 39**

San Nicolás de Tolentino

Hotel Los Cascajos (€)

This hotel makes a good stopping place if you want to take a break when driving around the island (► 44). Simple accommodation, with 20 rooms, plus a restaurant.

✉ **C/Los Cascajos 9** ☎ **928 89 11 65**

Santa Brígida

Hotel Escuela (€€)

In the cool hills of Monte Lentiscal, this hotel is a training school as well as a fully functioning hotel with a splendid dining room, gardens and pool; it enjoys an excellent reputation.

✉ **C/Real de Coello 2, Santa Brigida** ☎ **828 01 04 00**

Hotel Golf de Bandama (€€€)

A small country house/golf hotel on the edge of the Bandama crater, just 15m from the first hole. Most rooms have views of the course and the pool.

✉ **Bandama s/n** ☎ **928 35 15 38**

Tejeda

El Refugio (€€)

A rural hotel with 10 double rooms decorated in Canarian style. Good base for a walking holiday.

✉ **Cruz de Tejeda s/n** ☎ **928 66 65 13**

Getting around

You can stay in Las Palmas and still enjoy a visit to the southern resorts or to the centre and north by taking one of the buses run by Global Salcai Utinsa ☎ 902 38 11 10. The bus terminal is at Parque San Telmo, Las Palmas, information ☎ 928 36 83 35. Always double check bus numbers before making a journey. If you intend to travel a lot by bus on the island the Tarejeta Insular card might be worth considering. It gives 12 worth of travel at a 30 per cent discount. For further details contact the bus station in Las Palmas.

Traditional Stay

Located in the centre of Vega de San Mateo, La Cantonera (€€–€€€) ✉ Avda Tinamar 17 ☎ 928 66 17 95, forms part of a complex containing a museum of Canarian culture and a restaurant serving the best of Canarian cuisine. The rooms are tastefully furnished in rustic style and the whole setting is tranquil and pleasant. There is horse riding near by.

Las Palmas

Opening Hours
Shops open from 10 to 1:30 or 2, and from 4:30 to 8. When they are shut, they are very shut: that is, boarded up, so even window shopping is impossible. The department store El Corte Ingles on Avenida Mesa y Lopez in Las Palmas is open all day. It holds enough stock to satisfy the most compulsive consumer, until everything else opens again after lunch.

Shopping Malls
If it is shopping centres you want try Las Arenas at the west end of Las Canteras beach. On three levels, with parking below, it caters for a wide range of tastes, from fashion to traditional gifts, from books to jewellery. There are plenty of restaurants plus sea views. El Muelle in the port area has many well-known fashion outlets including Benetton, Zara and Timberland. It also has restaurants, bars, a cinema with 11 screens and discos on the top level. The biggest centre is at La Ballena, 3km out of town on the road to Teror, complete with hypermarket and more than 100 shops.

The best places to shop in Las Palmas are the streets around the Parque Santa Catalina and in the Triana district, particularly the pedestrianised Calle Mayor de Triana and the small streets off it.

Books

La Librería
The best bookshop in Las Palmas is run by the island government and stocks a wide range, including interesting material about Gran Canaria, books on flora and fauna and guide books.
✉ C/Cano 24 ☎ 928 38 15 39

Department Stores

El Corte Inglés
The only large department store on the island is on both sides of the street. You can buy anything from cheese to perfume, clothes, furniture and books. Ten-minute bus-ride from old town.
✉ Avda Mesa y Lopez 18
☎ 928 26 30 00

Marks & Spencer
Las Palmas' main branch of the international store.
✉ Avda Mesa y Lopez 32
☎ 928 26 35 83

Electronic Goods

Maya
A reputable chain of retailers dealing in cameras, videos, TVs, mobile phones, software etc. Also sunglasses and jewellery.
✉ C/Mayor de Triana 107
☎ 928 37 12 55 ✉ Buenos Aires 4 ☎ 928 36 93 91

Visanta
Do not try to bargain at this well-established electronic store. Prices are fixed and goods are guaranteed. There is another branch on C/29 de Abril and in the Yumbo Centrum, Playa del Inglés.
✉ C/Ripoche 25
☎ 928 27 17 14

Fashion

Boutique Gema
Modern clothes for young women.
✉ C/Travieso 13
☎ 928 36 27 79

Boutique Ibio
Smart Canarios, both ladies and gentlemen, favour this fashion store, particularly for Gucci accessories.
✉ C/ Viera y Clavijo 6
☎ 928 36 09 80

Zara
High fashion geared to young tastes. There are several other branches in the city.
✉ C/Mayor de Triana 39
☎ 928 38 27 32

Food and Drink

Cumbres Canarías
This deli stocks sausages and cheeses produced from all parts of the island, as well as take-away snacks and sandwiches.
✉ Tomás Miller 47–49
☎ 928 47 22 46

La Garriga
For all your deli products.
✉ C/Alvarado 16
☎ 928 37 17 10

Morales
A traditional *pasteleria* selling delicious cakes and pastries.
✉ C/Viera y Clavijo 4
☎ 928 36 06 35

Handicrafts

FEDAC

The Fundación para la Etnografía y el Desarollo de la Artesania Canaria is a non-profit public trust for the development of Canarian handicrafts and has two outlets on the island. This branch in Las Palmas sells decoratively carved bone-handled knives (naifes), pottery, traditional musical instruments and basketwork. A woman spins wool by the door to create an artisan ambience. This is the place to contact if you are interested in Canarian crafts throughout the island.

✉ C/Domingo J Navarro 7
☎ 928 36 96 61; www.fedac.org

Orbis

Sr Miguel Santana Cruz specialises in timples, a type of small Canarian guitar. Buy off the peg, or get one custom-made.

✉ C/Mayor de Triana 51
☎ 928 36 81 48

Higmara

The speciality of the shop is embroidered shawls in all colours and designs.

✉ 22 León y Castillo
☎ 928 36 63 38

Markets

Mercado de Vegueta

The oldest general market in the city, where you can find fish, meat, fruit and vegetables – the variety of potatoes is astonishing. The market is surrounded by small lively bars and churrerías – stalls selling churros fritters (a traditional Spanish breakfast).

✉ C/Mendizábal

Mercado del Puerto

Popular with sailors from ships docked in port. Like most Canarian markets, it stays open 7AM until 2PM.

✉ C/Albareda

Mercado de Las Flores

Arts, crafts and flower market held on Sunday mornings in the attractive old city square.

✉ Plaza de Santo Domingo

Perfumes

Defa

Offers a good selection of cosmetics and perfumes. All the major brands are here.

✉ C/Galicia 27 (also at C/Cano 4 and C/Tajaraste 4) ☎ 928 26 82 18

Maya

Another Maya store, this one selling a good range of perfumes and cosmetics.

✉ C/Mayor de Triana 105
☎ 928 37 20 49

Yves Rocher

A huge range of perfumes and beauty goods at very reasonable prices.

✉ C/Nestor de la Torre 36
☎ 928 24 73 89

Tobacco

Marquez

Cigars and cigarettes of all lengths and thicknesses, including those from the island of La Palma, said to be the best among the Canaries.

✉ C/Ripoche 1 ☎ 928 26 56 35

Added Value?

It is no longer true that the Canary Islands are a duty-free haven for bargain-hunters. Admittedly there is no value added tax and there are some minor concessions based on Spain's terms of entry into the European Union. However, these factors do not automatically guarantee low prices. Check out the supermarkets for good prices.

The South

Resort Shopping

Shopping can be a bizarre experience in the southern resorts because, with the exception of Puerto de Mogán, the activity is concentrated in the giant shopping/restaurant/ entertainment malls called *centros comerciales*, rather than in shops on streets. These shopping centres are often huge concrete blocks three to four storeys high, connected by stairs and passages. The shops themselves, with one or two exceptions, appear rather tatty and generally stock a limited range of cheap goods.

Centros Comerciales

Maspalomas
Faro 2
Regarded as the most up-market in the whole San Agustín/Playa del Inglés/ Maspalomas complex. Faro 2 is one of three centres in Maspalomas, the others being Oasis and Veradero, the latter featuring stores such as Chanel, Diesel and Lacoste.
✉ **Avenida Touroperador Holland, Maspalomas** ☎ **928 76 91 97**

Playa del Inglés
Yumbo Centrum
This is the biggest commercial centre in the resort. Other centres are Aguila Roja, Alohe, Anexo 11, Cita, El Veril, Gran Chaparral, Kasbah; La Sandia, Metro, Plaza de Maspalomas and Tropical.
✉ **Avenida de Los Estados Unidos 54** ☎ **928 76 41 96**

San Agustín
San Agustín
A large commercial centre on three floors. There is a smaller one called El Pulpo.
✉ **C/de las Dalias**

San Fernando
San Fernando
Along with Botánico, the Mercado Municipal, Nilo and Eurocenter, this is an economical place to shop.
✉ **Avenida de Tejeda**

Handicrafts

Playa del Inglés/Maspalomas
Tienda FEDAC
All manner of Canarian handcrafted items on sale here. Products include work in clay, wool, linen and iron.
✉ **Avenida de España/Avenida de los Estados Unidos**
☎ **928 77 24 45**

La Galería
A shop in the great warren of the Yumbo Centro carrying a range of island handicrafts, as well as from further afield. There are occasional gems to be discovered here.
✉ **Yumbo Centro, Playa del Inglés** ☎ **928 76 41 96**

FEDAC
Canarian handicrafts sold at the Tourist Information Office. Fedac's aim is to maintain and develop traditional crafts. The items on sale are guaranteed to be genuine Canarian craftsmanship and not foreign replicas.
✉ **Centro Insular de Turismo, Avenida de España (on corner with Avenida de los Estados Unidos), Playa del Inglés**

Puerto de Mogán
La Bodeguilla Juananá
A craft shop-cum-restaurant selling the best – that is, the most authentic Canarian produce, be it ceramic bowls or local cheeses, well displayed. Open 12–4 and 7–midnight, unless the owner has gone fishing, when he leaves a notice on the window to that effect. During summer months, open evenings only. Closed Mon. The restaurant serves nouvelle Canarian cuisine, a far cry from the usual hearty stews.
✉ **Puerto de Mogán, local 390**
☎ **928 56 50 44**

Candle Palace
Candles made on the premises in all shapes and sizes.

✉ **Puerto de Mogán, local 139**
☎ **928 72 52 01**

Rincon Canario
This stylishly decorated shop stocks a wide range of Canarian handicrafts including ceramics, embroidery, basketwork.

✉ **Puerto de Mogán, local 105**
☎ **928 56 40 44**

Markets

Arguineguín
Fish market
Held every morning. There is also a general market on Tuesday and Thursday.

✉ **Arguineguín harbour**

Puerto de Mogán
Fish market
Another daily fish market. Friday is the general market day. Open 10–2.

✉ **Puerto de Mogán harbour**

Playa del Inglés
Monday to Saturday
An evening craft market held in the Plaza de Maspalomas next to the mini-train. Good for presents. Open 6–11.

✉ **Plaza de Masplomas**

San Fernando
Wednesday and Saturday markets
A wide range of local goods on sale. Open 8–2.

✉ **Avenida Alejandro del Castillo s/n**

Vecindario
Wednesday market
A variety of products sold on the weekly stalls. Open 8–2.

✉ **Avenida de Canarias**

Needlework and Embroidery

Ingenio
Museo de Piedras y Artesania Canaria
Needlework and embroidery from Gran Canaria and the rest of the archipelago as well as basketwork, pottery, herbs, straw hats, pearls, leather, jewellery and cigars. There are also dolls in traditional costume. An interesting range of products made from natural plants featuring the aloe vera plant is used in cosmetics and other local plants have been used in the manufacture of perfume.

✉ **Camino Real de Gando 1**
☎ **928 78 11 24**

Pottery

Ingenio
Taller Almagre
Look here for Canarian pottery – hand-turned and unglazed.

✉ **La Capellanía 18**
☎ **928 78 27 47**

Mogán
Miguel Hernandez
Traditional pottery 10km inland from Puerto de Mogán.

✉ **El Horno 8** ☎ **928 15 90 72**

Bargain Buys
Nobody will be surprised if you bargain over the prices quoted for goods on sale in the *centros comerciales*. You can take the opportunity to haggle over items such as perfumes, leather goods – bags and coats, T-shirts, towels, tablecloths, baseball caps and clothes and electronic products, sold in establishments often owned by Asian traders, known locally as *Hindoos*.

Central & North Gran Canaria

Canarian Music

The *timple* is a small four- or five-stringed Canarian guitar and the *chacara* is the Canarian castanet – both are handcrafted on the island. Since the revival of folk music on the island in the 1970s, traditional music and dance have acquired a special importance. You will find the music of Gran Canaria's most popular folk group, Los Gofiones, in any music shop.

Food and Drink

Arucas
Destilerías Arehucas

Come here for rum, famous produce of Arucas. You can see barrels signed by King Juan Carlos and Tom Jones and then have a free tasting of both rum and liqueurs. Some of the rums have been aged for up to 12 years. If it is rum-based liqueurs you prefer take your pick from banana, orange, coffee, almond or honey.

✉ **Lugar Era de San Pedro 2**
☎ **928 62 49 00**

Moya
Doramas

Mouthwatering biscuits and cakes, including the traditional *mimos* and *suspiros*.

✉ **C/General Franco 19**
☎ **928 62 00 80**

San Bartolomé de Tirajana
Bar Martin

Guindilla, liqueur made from sour cherries, is on sale at this bar.

✉ **C/Reyes Catolicos**

Bodega Vino Tinto

Attractively laid-out shop with a variety of local produce from the island, with a leaning towards Canarian wines.

✉ **C/Reyes Católicos**

Santa María de Guía
Los Quesos

A cheese emporium, assorted produce of sheep and goat's milk along with honey, local wine, rum and a good variety of craftwork.

✉ **Carretera General Lomo de Guillén, Santa María de Guía**

Santiago Gil Romero/El Camino de Gilmani SL

Buy *queso de flor de Guía*, a creamy cheese flavoured with artichoke flowers. Cheese in this fascinating relic of a shop is left to mature on bamboo mats.

✉ **C/Marqués de Muni 34**
☎ **928 88 18 75**

Tejeda
Dulcería Nublo

Delicious almond sweets and cakes. It is well known for its *mazapan* (almond cake).

✉ **C/Dr Hernández Guerra**
☎ **928 66 60 30**

Handicrafts

Arucas

There are several traditional craftsmen working in and around Arucas. It's worth exploring the little shops selling embroidery, jewellery and carvings in wood and stone.

Feluco

Small sculptures and objects made of the grey basalt stone, *piedra azul*, from local quarries. Picture frames, flowers, a model of the church of San Juan Bautista in Arucas – are all sold here.

✉ **C/Dr Fleming** ☎ **928 60 54 45**

Roberto Ramirez

This is the place for walking sticks that are not just functional but carved, sculpted, inlaid, bound and decorated until they become collectors' pieces; and for extravagantly fanciful kites.

✉ **C/ Mateos 9**
☎ **928 60 14 65**

Fataga
Artesanía Canaria

An opportunity to buy some

genuine Canarian products made from simple and pure materials including clay, wool, linen and iron. Two branches in the town.

✉ **Parque Doramas**
☎ **928 24 39 11**

Gáldar
Tabaiba

All sorts of traditional handicrafts and locally made goods are sold here.

✉ **Capitán Quesada 22**
☎ **928 88 32 82**

Gáldar, Guía and Telde

Traditional craftsmen in these villages make *Cuchillos Canarios* (Canarian knives), an essential tool for every Canarian farmer and valuable collectors' pieces, due to their decorated handles.

La Atalaya
Centro Locero

This village has long been a centre of pottery production. There is a strong sense of preserving traditional techniques and the ALUD (Association of Professionals of La Loza of La Atalaya) has a programme of continued research and teaching as well as organising the exhibition and sale of items of pottery. Through their work they are passing knowledge on to a new generation.

✉ **Camino de la Picota 11**
☎ **928 28 82 70**

Santa María de Guía
Juan JoséCaballero Rodriguez

Juan Jose Caballero works in wood – traditional country tools and objects – bowls, spoons, boxes and stools. He also stocks antiques –

and virtually anything else, in fact, as long as it is fashioned out of wood.

✉ **C/Lepanto 9** ☎ **928 88 27 79**

Tafira
La Calzada

Located on the right-hand side of the road leading to the Jardín Botánico Canairo at Tafira Baja, this artisan shop sells a variety of goods made in Gran Canaria.

✉ **Tafira Baja**
☎ **No phone**

Markets

Arucas
Saturday market

A busy weekly market, held, as in all major towns, in addition to the permanent municipal market.

✉ **Plaza de la Constitución**

Santa Brígida
Saturday and Sunday market

Lively small open-air market near the car park. Lots of local fruit, vegetables and flowers, as well as an interesting selection of cheeses, cakes and honey.

✉ **C/Dieciocho**

Teror
Sunday market

A fascinating selection of local produce, including marzipan cakes from the nearby convent, and the town's very own sausage, *chorizo rojo*.

✉ **Plaza del Pino**

Vega de San Mateo
Sunday market

Situated in the centre of a richly agricultural community, this market attracts customers from all over the island.

✉ **Avenida del Mercado**

Ceramics

Most of the ceramics sold on the island are made in the traditional manner and to traditional designs. These are generally simple objects of everyday use like bowls, plates or jugs. Occasionally you will find copies of pre-Hispanic artefacts, such as the terracotta Mother Earth-type idol figure (the *Ídolo de Tara*), clay pipes (*cachimbas*), or seals in geometric patterns (*pintaderas*), now fashioned into brooches or pins.

Las Palmas & the South

Central Gran Canaria and the North

Any trip to a cave church or a restaurant in a cave (Artenara) is at least a novelty for young people, but there is not much to entertain children in the north or centre, with the exception of Reptilandia in Gáldar (✉ Carretera Norte ☎ 928 55 12 69), where poisonous snakes, alligators, lizards and turtles can be seen in a pleasant hillside park, plus a parrot on a perch that calls out 'Hola. Que tal?' ('Hi. How are you?'), as you approach.

Las Palmas
Casa de Colón
Children who are intrigued by adventure, exploration and ships will love this house where Christopher Columbus once stayed (➤ 18 and 31).
✉ Calle de Colón 1 ☎ 928 31 23 73 🕐 Mon–Fri 9–7, Sat–Sun 9–3. Closed public hols 🚌 30 from Maspalomas, 1 from Parque Santa Catalina

Museo Canario
A museum full of mummies, skulls and skeletons should be a hit with children (➤ 33).
✉ Calle Dr Verneau 2 ☎ 928 33 68 00 🕐 Mon–Fri 10–8, Sat–Sun 10–2. Closed public hols 🚌 30 from Maspalomas, 1 from Parque Santa Catalina

Museo Elder
State-of-the-art museum of science and technology, the majority of the exhibits are interactive. IMAX cinema. Fun for all the family (➤ 33).
✉ Parque Santa Catalina s/n 35007 ☎ 828 01 18 28 🕐 Tue–Sun 10–8 (summer 11–9). Closed Mon & some public hols 🚌 1, 2, 3

Parque Doramas
Another green space where you can let the children off the leash (➤ 36). They can watch Canarian folk dancing in the Pueblo Canario and remember the sad fate of the early Guanches evoked in the statue outside the Hotel Santa Catalina.
✉ Ciudad Jardín 🚌 1

Parque San Telmo
There is a children's recreation area in this park (➤ 38), and children might enjoy the tiles and curves of the popular kiosk café.

✉ Corner of Calle Bravo Murillo and Avenida Rafael Cabrera 🚌 1, 11, 41

Parque Santa Catalina
If you are visiting the city during any of the fiestas, particularly if you are here at Carnival, take the children to the special children's shows here, early each evening. There is music, dancing, laser shows and entertainments on a huge stage (➤ 38).
✉ Santa Catalina ☎ Tourist Information Office 928 26 46 23 🚌 1, 2, 3

Playa de las Canteras
A child-friendly beach is an advantage in a city where few entertainments are especially provided for children (➤ 23 and 39).
✉ Las Palmas ☎ Tourist Information Office at Parque Santa Catalina 928 26 46 23 🚌 1, 2, 3, 20, 21

Agüimes
Cocodrilo Park
The largest collection of crocodiles in Europe can be seen in this park, 28km northwest of Playa del Inglés. Other animals are housed here, many rescued from cruelty and neglect, including a family of Bengal tigers. Crocodile and other shows throughout the day. Buses from main southern resorts and Las Palmas; enquire at local tourist office.
✉ Carretera Gral Los Corralillos km 5.5, Villa de Agüimes ☎ 928 78 47 25 🕐 10–6

Maspalomas
Aquasur
Day-long fun in pools and water slides, at this very popular water park (➤ 47).

☒ Mte. León, Carretera Palmitos Parque km 3 ☎ 928 14 19 82 ⏰ Daily, summer 10–6, winter 10–5 🚌 45, 70 from Maspolamas

Camello Safari Dunas
A camel ride is always popular, and an even bigger treat when through sand dunes. Don't forget the sun hats. Camel safaris are also available in the Fataga and Arteara (► 47).

☒ Avenida Dunas s/n, Isla de Lobos 70, San Fernando ☎ 928 76 07 81 ⏰ Daily 9–4:30 🚌 Plaza del Faro, 29, 30, 32

Holiday World
Everything for a great evening out for the family – roller coasters, roundabouts, arcades and plenty of restaurants (► 47).

☒ Carretera General Las Palmas ☎ 928 73 04 98 ⏰ Sun–Thu 9–2, Fri–Sat 9–6 🚌 45, 70 from Maspalomas

Palmitos Parque
Although children love the performing parrots, this is much more than a parrot park. There is a great aquarium and snack bars and cafés serving hamburgers and pizzas.

☒ Barranco de Chamoriscán ☎ 928 14 02 76 ⏰ Daily 10–6 🚌 Free bus from Maspalomas; 45 , 70 from Maspalomas

Playa del Inglés
Mini-Tren
This miniature train covers a circular route at Playa del Inglés starting, and finishing, at the El Veril Comercial Centre on Avenida Italia. It gives legs a rest while revealing a different view of the world. The train usually leaves every 30 minutes for

a 30-minute trip.The service is run privately and depends on the operator's mood.

Puerto de Mogán
Submarine Adventure
Journey to the bottom of the sea – well, almost. A submarine trip to see a wreck and brilliant marine life (► 57).

☒ Pantalán Dique Sur ☎ 928 56 51 08 ⏰ 10, 11, 12, 1, 2, 3:30, 4:20, 5:10 🚌 Free bus from resorts

Puerto Rico
Escuela de Vela J Blanco
Sailing courses for groups or individuals; also boat trips.

☒ Playa de Puerto Rico ☎ 677 70 49 81 (information); 928 29 15 67 (reservations: Federacíon de la Vela)

Spirit of the Sea
Enjoy a 2-hour dolphin search aboard this glass-bottomed catamaran with underwater microphones and cameras. You might even spot a whale! Part of the ticket price goes to research.

☒ Puerto Rico Harbour ☎ 928 56 22 29 ⏰ 10, 12:30, 3

San Agustín
Gran Karting Club
Not just for adults or big kids, this go-kart track – the largest in Spain – even caters for children under five (► 62).

☒ Carretera General del Sur km 46 ☎ 928 15 71 90 ⏰ Daily, summer 11–10, winter 10–9

Sioux City
Wild West show with enough jail break-outs, gun-chases, bows and arrows and bullets (fake) for any young person (► 63).

☒ Cañón del Águila ☎ 928 76 25 73 ⏰ 10–5. Closed Mon 🚌 Salcai bus 29

Bull-friendly Fights
A special tourist-geared bullfight takes place every Thursday in Playa del Inglés, when the bull is not harmed (bullfighting is not as popular on the Canary Islands as it is on the mainland).

Las Palmas

Nightlife in Las Palmas
There is something in this city for every taste, however mainstream or bizarre. The general rule is: the nearer you are to the Parque Santa Catalina and the later at night, the nearer you are to topless bars, sex shows and to nightlife of a generally *louche* nature. That is not to suggest, however, that there are no wild night-time entertainments in the Old Town or that you will not find a quiet place to sip a mineral water in a Santa Catalina bar. The venues for young nightlife change with every season. The signs are that the trendiest clubs are in the Las Arenas *centro comercial* and around the marina at Las Palmas. If you turn up at a bar or disco before 10PM, you will find yourself alone.

Films

The International Film Festival of Las Palmas de Gran Canaria has been running since 1999 and is held in March in the Alfredo Kraus Auditorium (▶ 113) – for exact dates contact the tourist office – and has as many as 14 countries competing for a range of awards for 'best of,' for example, directors, short films, photography etc.

Multicines La Ballena
Based in the shopping and entertainment complex by the southern exit out of town. Mostly foreign and dubbed mainstream films.
✉ La Ballena Centro Comercial ☎ 928 42 03 35

Multicines Las Arenas
Located in Las Arenas shopping mall, at the west end of Las Canteras beach.
✉ Carretera del Rincón s/n
☎ 928 27 70 08

Multicines Monopol
Another option in the Galeria de Arte Monopol (▶ this page), in the student quarter of the old town.
✉ Plaza de Mendoza s/n
☎ 928 36 74 38

Multicines Royal
A choice of screens and mainstream films.
✉ C/León y Castillo 40
☎ 928 36 09 54

Warner
Located in the El Muelle shopping centre near the port, this is a good venue to see the latest releases.
✉ El Muelle de Santa Catalina s/n ☎ No phone; see local newspapers for information

Folk Dancing

Pueblo Canario
Many cultures have contributed to the folk dancing styles of Gran Canaria, not least the Spanish, Portuguese and Latin American. The *isa* is a lively, energetic dance, the *folia*, slower and more languorous, *el canario*, a group dance, and all are accompanied by music played on traditional instruments, once a week in the Canarian Village. The folk costumes, now worn on rare formal occasions, differ from village to village, but they are all splendidly colourful.
✉ Parque Doramas
☎ 928 24 29 85
🕐 Performances Sun 11:30AM
🚌 1

For Students

Galeria de Arte Monopol
For students and the young this small shopping centre, close to the old town, draws a crowd at night. It is in a pleasant square opposite the Biblioteca (library) and has many outdoor tables. Inside are bars and cafés, fashion and art outlets and a multi-screen cinema (▶ this page).
✉ Plaza de Hurtado de Mendoza/calle San Pedro
☎ 677 53 53 26

Nightclubs and Bars

Bachira
Loud and popular fashionable venue with house and dance music.
✉ Centro Comercial Plaza, Playa del Inglés
🕐 All night

Camel Bar
Calle León y Castillo is a popular club venue not far from the old part of the city. You can take a meal before dancing the night away.

✉ C/León y Castillo 389
☎ 928 27 23 06
🕐 Mon–Sat 9PM–4AM

Casino de las Palmas
The smartest place on the island to risk your fortune, or watch someone else risk theirs on black jack, *chemin de fer*, baccarat, roulette, etc. Formal dress obligatory. Take your passport.

✉ Santa Catalina Hotel, Parque Doramas ☎ 928 23 39 08 ;
www.casinolaspalmas.com
🕐 Sun–Thu 8PM–4AM, Fri–Sat 8PM–5AM

El Coto
As you would expect of a discothèque in the Hotel Melia, the ambience is elegant and the atmosphere refined – even on a Saturday night. The music is international/Latin American.

✉ C/Gomera 6 ☎ 928 26 76 00

Floridita
A large popular restaurant/bar in the Triana district. Locals love the Cuban ambience and rhythm.

✉ C/Remedios 10–12
☎ 928 43 17 40

GUASQUEAS
Smart and lively venue for all age groups to see and hear top performers. Good jazz and Latin American music.

✉ C/San Pedro 2, near Triana
☎ 928 37 00 46
🕐 From 10:30PM–late

Heaven
Gay and straight dance club with a hot reputation.

✉ Third Floor, Yumbo Centre, Maspalomas 🕐 All night

Pacha
Smart, popular disco that's been around a while. Giant video screen and live music on the terrace.

✉ Avenida Provisionales 10, Playa del Inglés
☎ 928 76 81 77

Theatre and Concerts

Auditorio Alfredo Kraus
A major venue for classical music concerts and a conference centre right on the beach with great sea views.

✉ Paseo de las Canteras s/n
☎ 928 49 17 70;
www.auditorio-alfredokraus.com 🕐 Ticket office: Mon–Fri,10–2, 4:30–8:30, Sat 10–2

Teatro Cuyás
This theatre opened in 2000 in a former cinema in Triana and hosts a range of productions from drama, comedy and ballet.

✉ C/Viera y Clavijo s/n
☎ 928 43 21 81;
www.teatrocuyas.com
🚌 1

Teatro Pérez Galdós
Home to the island's symphony orchestra and operatic society, the theatre also hosts visits from groups, orchestras and performers of international standing. Closed for restoration at the time of writing, but the building is well worth a look.

✉ C/Lentini 1
☎ 928 36 15 09 🚌 1

Music, Ballet, Opera and Theatre
An International Music Festival is held every year in Las Palmas, in January and early February. March and April see the Festival of Opera, and in July the International Festival of Ballet and Dance is celebrated, including performances of Spanish light opera called *zarzuelas*.

The South, Centre & North

Disco Life
Discos, pubs and nightlife in general are concentrated in the *centros comerciales* – the commercial centres, of which there are many in the southern resorts. German and British entertainers often perform in bars and pubs to their own national clientele. Centro Comercial Kasbah, Playa del Inglés, is the most popular for dancing or listening to music: try Meliá, Roger's, Beckham Bar or China White Costa. Centro Comercial Metro, Playa del Inglés, has a solid following among young people at Pachá and Joy. Centro Comercial Yumbo, Playa del Inglés, attracts a gay crowd to bars and discos like King's Club and Come Back.

Diving
Gran Canaria is an ideal place for scuba diving. For more information visit www.gran-canaria-diving.com

Nightlife

San Agustín
Casino Tamarindos Palace
You have to be over 18, look respectable (that is, wear jacket and tie if you are male) and carry identification to gamble or watch. Also a caberet show.

🖂 Hotel Tamarindos, C/Las Retamas 3, San Agustín
☎ 928 76 27 24

Sport

Diving
Arguineguín
Dive Academy
The most southerly dive centre in Europe and the only one in Gran Canaria with its own pool for tuition. Air-conditioned classrooms and dive shop. A PADI Gold Palm centre, safety is their number one concern.

🖂 Club Amigos del Atlantico C/Lajilla s/n
☎ 928 73 61 96

Puerto Rico
Aquanauts Dive Center
Run by a Finnish company which offers daily dives, night dives on Sun and Thu and full-day dives (two tanks) plus introductory courses for learners.

🖂 Commercial Centre, Puerto Base, Local 5, Sotano
☎ 928 56 06 55;
www.aquanauts-divecenter.com

San Agustín
Dive Center Nautico
This German firm offers courses for beginners and takes more experienced divers out into deep water.

🖂 IFA Club Atlantic, C/Los Jazmines 2 ☎ 928 77 81 68

Fishing
Puerto Rico
Barakuda Dos
Sport and high seas fishing trip; sandwiches and drinks provided plus tackle and bait. The skipper can give instruction in Spanish, English, French and German. Make a reservation at least two days ahead.

☎ 689 16 88 15;
www.barakudados.com
🕘 Daily 9AM–1PM

Golf
Arguineguín
Salobre Golf & Resort
Just off the the GC1 motorway near Arguineguín this course has fine views towards the sea and mountains. It is an 18-hole, par 71 course with additional driving range, putting green and restaurant.

🖂 Urbanización El Saobre
☎ 928 01 01 03

Caldera de Bandama
Club de Golf
Splendid location on the edge of the Bandama crater, near Santa Brígida: 18 holes, par 71, 5,679m course. Hotel and restaurant attached. Visitors, as temporary members, may play, except at weekends. Riding school attached (► 115).

🖂 Carretera de Bandama s/n
☎ 928 35 01 04 🚌 39

Maspalomas
Campo de Golf
Close to dunes and palm groves, this is another splendidly sited golf course: 18 holes, par 73, 6,220m course. Visitors may book lessons, hire clubs and practise on the driving range.

🖂 Avenida Neckerman s/n
☎ 928 76 25 81 🚌 30

Mountain Biking
Playa del Inglés
Happy Biking

Bike hire from one to six days, special weekend rates. Tours of varying difficulty; prices include hire of bike, helmet, gloves, picnic and insurance. Rollerblade hire.

✉ Hotel Continental, Avenida. de Italia 2 ☎ 928 76 68 32

Riding
Bandama
Bandama Golf Club Riding School

Associated with the golf club, this horse-riding school offers lessons and treks in a dramatic rural landscape.

✉ Carretera de Bandama s/n ☎ 928 35 10 50

Happy Horse

With an English guide you can go on 1- or 2-hour rides around the Palmitos valley or a 3-hour ride to the beach at Meloneras. Beginners and experienced riders welcome.

✉ Carretera Palmitos Park, Finca 9 ☎ 679 86 70 57

Sailing
Puerto de Mogán
Canrias Charters

Bare-boat hire of good quality yachts, or challenging trips with a professional skipper.

✉ C/Los Montiscos 6 ☎ 928 56 95 19; www.canariascharters.com

Tennis
Maspalomas
El Tenis Center Maspalomas

Situated in a fine setting, close to Maspalomas beach and in the heart of the Campo de Golf course, the tennis centre offers 11 clay courts and professional help when needed. You can also play squash and work out in the gym. There is a restaurant on site.

✉ Avenida Tour Operador Tjaereborj 9, Campo de Golf ☎ 928 76 74 47

Walking
Playa del Inglés
Canariaventura

Take a guided walk along the island's paths and get close to nature. You will be provided with water and snacks and even sticks if you need them. Departs Wednesdays at 9AM. Canariaventura also offer bungee-jumping, canyoning, kyaking and archery.

✉ C C Eurocenter, Planta 2, Local 29 ☎ 928 76 61 68; www.canariaventura.com

Windsurfing

Most beaches have equipment to hire and offer lessons to beginners and those wishing to improve their skills.

Playa del Águila
F2 Surfcenter Dunkerbeck

Eugen Dunkerbeck runs a windsurf school for beginners and provides facilities for those with advanced skills.

✉ Plaza de Hibiscus, Águila Playa ☎ 928 76 29 58

Name-calling

Canarios consider themselves to be different from mainland Spaniards, whom they call 'Peninsulares'. Occasionally, when they feel less than kind, they refer to them as 'Godos' or Goths. You may see signs saying: 'Afuera Godos' – 'Goths Go Home'.

Island Walkers

Walking in the mountains is a popular activity on Gran Canaria, particularly with the younger generation. Older folk remember a time when there were few roads on the island and walking was the only method of transport. Not surprisingly, they prefer to ride in motorcars. Caminos Reales, literally 'royal ways', are a network of paths once guaranteed by royal authority. They now form the basis of much of the island's walking tracks.

What's On When

Festivals

Gran Canaria has a wealth of festivals. Before Carnival is the Almond Blossom Festival; after Carnival is Holy Week. Then there are the anniversaries of the Spanish conquest, the ancient aboriginal festivities and the great island pilgrimage to Teror. That's not counting all the festivals associated with the produce of the earth – of *gofio*, apricots – and the sea, and the celebrations of the saints' days of each town and village. San Juan, held in Las Palmas in June is the most important cultural event on the island.

January

Festival of the Three Kings, 6 January: gifts for the children.

February

Almond Blossom Festival, Tejeda and Valsequillo: song and dance, picnics, almond sweets and cakes.
Carnival: street bands, parties and parades.

March

Arguineguín celebrates the feast day of Santa Agueda.

March/April

Semana Santa is celebrated during Holy Week throughout the island. Processions with sacred icons and religious sculptures take place.

Late May/early June

Feast of Corpus Christi (sometimes in May): the streets are decorated with flowers and sand.
Anniversary of the foundation of Las Palmas. During this festival, known as San Juan, a large number of cultural events take place in the city. Music, dance and theatre performances abound.

July

Fiestas del Carmen are celebrated by all fishing villages, 16 July.
Feast day of Santiago, 25 July, Gáldar and San Bartolomé. Gáldar has Canarian wrestling, *romerias* (picnics) and traditional dancing.

August

Bajada de la Rama celebrated in Agaete, 4 August, is probably the most popular festival on the island. From an ancient aboriginal rite of praying for rain. Local people climbed high into the pine forests and brought down branches to thrash the sea. Modern Canarios do the same. This is a great opportunity to get wet and have a party.

September

Feast of La Virgen del Pino (Our Lady of the Pine) in Teror, the patron saint of the whole island, 8 September. Pilgrims come from all over the island, many of them walking through the night to Teror. They may bring cartfuls of produce, which are placed before the image of the Virgin in the square and then dispensed to poor folk later. Fiesta del Charco in San Nicolás de Tolentino, 10 September.

October

Fiestas de Nuestra Señora del Rosario (Our Lady of the Rosary), celebrated in Agüimes, 5 October, with Canarian stick-fighting and wrestling.
La Naval, 6 October in Las Palmas, commemorates the successful repulsion of the English privateer, Francis Drake in 1595.
Fiesta de la Manza on the first Sunday in October celebrates the apple harvest with a festival in Valleseco, near Teror.

November

Festival of San Martín de Porres, Arinaga.

December

Fiesta de los Labradores, Santa Lucía, 20 December: people celebrate by dressing in peasant costume and carrying old-fashioned farming tools.

Practical Matters

Above: *keeping a cool head at Barranco de Guayadeque*
Right: *exquisite example of Gran Canarian flora*

117

TIME DIFFERENCES

GMT	Gran Canaria	Germany	USA (NY)	Netherlands	Spain
12 noon	12 noon	1PM	7AM	1PM	1PM

BEFORE YOU GO

WHAT YOU NEED

- ● Required
- ○ Suggested
- ▲ Not required

Some countries require a passport to remain valid for a minimum period (usually at least six months) beyond the date of entry – contact their consulate or embassy or your travel agent for details.

	UK	Germany	USA	Netherlands	Spain
Passport/National Identity Card	●	●	●	●	▲
Visa (regulations can change – check before you travel)	▲	▲	▲	▲	▲
Onward or Return Ticket	▲	▲	▲	▲	▲
Health Inoculations	▲	▲	▲	▲	▲
Health Documentation (➤ 123, Health)	●	●	●	●	▲
Travel Insurance	○	○	○	○	○
Driving Licence (national or international; Spain national only)	●	●	●	●	●
Car Insurance Certificate (if own car)	●	●	●	●	●
Car Registration Document (if own car)	●	●	●	●	●

WHEN TO GO

Gran Canaria

High season

Low season

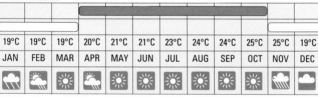

JAN	FEB	MAR	APR	MAY	JUN	JUL	AUG	SEP	OCT	NOV	DEC
Low	Low	Low	High	High	High	High	High	High	High	Low	Low
19°C	19°C	19°C	20°C	21°C	21°C	23°C	24°C	24°C	25°C	25°C	19°C
Wet	Sunshine & showers	Sun	Sunshine & showers	Sun	Sun	Sun	Sun	Sun	Sun	Very wet	Cloud

Very wet · Wet · Cloud · Sun · Sunshine & showers

TOURIST OFFICES

In the UK
SpanishTourist Office
79 New Cavendish Street
London W1W 6XB
☎ 0207 486 8077
Fax: 0207 486 8034

In the USA
Tourist Office of Spain
666 Fifth Avenue 35th
New York
NY 10103
☎ 212/265 8822
Fax: 212/265 8864

Tourist Office of Spain
8383 Wilshire Boulevard
Suite 960
Beverly Hills
Cal 90211
☎ 323/658 7195
Fax: 323/658 1061

LOCAL POLICE 112 or 092

FIRE 112 or 080 (Las Palmas)

AMBULANCE 112 or 061

HOSPITAL 928 45 00 00 (Las Palmas)

WHEN YOU ARE THERE

ARRIVING

Most visitors arrive on charter flights direct from western Europe. Visitors from North America may have to fly via Madrid. There is a weekly car ferry service from the Spanish mainland (Cádiz) taking 36 hours, operated by Trasmediterránea (☎ 902 45 46 45 on Gran Canaria).

Gando Airport Kilometres to Las Palmas	Journey times
	🚉 N/A
22 kilometres	🚌 20 minutes
	🚗 15 minutes

Puerto de la Luz Ferry Terminal Kilometres to Las Palmas	Journey times
	🚉 N/A
3 kilometres	🚌 10 minutes
	🚗 5 minutes

MONEY

The euro is the single currency of the European Monetary Union, which has been adopted by 12 member states including Spain. Euro banknotes and coins were introduced in January 2002. There are banknotes for 5, 10, 20, 50, 100, 200 and 500 euros, and coins for 1, 2, 5, 10, 20 and 50 cents, and 1 and 2 euros. Euro traveller's cheques are widely accepted.

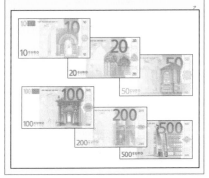

TIME

 Gran Canaria, like the rest of the Canaries, is in the same time zone as the UK, which is 1 hour behind the EU. The islands change to Summer Time (GMT+1) on the same date as the UK and the rest of the EU. The Canaries are therefore 1 hour behind mainland Spain and 5 hours ahead of the

CUSTOMS

 YES

As the Canaries are a free-trade zone there are no limits on the amounts of alcohol, tobacco, perfume, toilet water and other goods (except for gifts of value greater than €48) that can be brought into the Islands, but the prices of these products are so low in the Canaries that it seems a pointless exercise to do so. Visitors may bring an unlimited amount of Spanish or foreign currency in to the Canaries but should declare any amount exceeding the equivalent of €6,000 to avoid difficulties on leaving.

NO

Drugs, firearms, ammunition, offensive weapons, obscene material, unlicensed animals.

CONSULATES

UK
928 26 25 08

Germany
928 49 18 80

USA
928 22 25 52

Netherlands
928 36 22 51

WHEN YOU ARE THERE

TOURIST OFFICES

- Patronato de Turismo Gran Canaria (Local Tourist Authority)
  León y Castillo 17
  35003 Las Palmas de Gran Canaria
  ☎ 928 21 96 00
  Fax: 928 21 96 01
  www.grancanaria.com

- Oficina de Turismo Las Palmas
  Las Palmas de Gran Canaria
  ☎ 928 44 68 24

- Centro Insular de Turismo (Tourism Insular Centre)
  Centro Commercial Yumbo
  Playa del Inglés
  ☎ 928 77 15 50

- Avda de Mogán Puerto
  Puerto Rico
  ☎ 928 15 88 04;
  www.mogan.es

- Oficina Municipal de Turismo de Agüimes
  Plaza de San Anton 1
  ☎ 928 12 41 83

Most towns and some larger villages throughout Gran Canaria have a local tourist office. Times of opening vary and most close for the weekend.

NATIONAL HOLIDAYS

J	F	M	A	M	J	J	A	S	O	N	D
2		2	1	3	1		1	1	1	1	3

1 Jan	New Year's Day
6 Jan	Epiphany
19 Mar	St Joseph's Day
Mar/Apr	Maundy Thu, Good Fri and Easter Mon
1 May	Labour Day
30 May	Canary Island Day
May/Jun	Corpus Christi
15 Aug	Assumption of the Virgin
8 Sep	Birthday of the Virgin Mary
12 Oct	National Day
1 Nov	All Saints' Day
6 Dec	Constitution Day
8 Dec	Feast of the Immaculate Conception
25 Dec	Christmas Day

Most shops, offices and museums close on these days.

OPENING HOURS

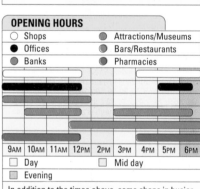

○ Shops   ● Attractions/Museums
● Offices   ● Bars/Restaurants
● Banks   ● Pharmacies

| 9AM | 10AM | 11AM | 12PM | 2PM | 3PM | 4PM | 5PM | 6PM |

☐ Day   ☐ Mid day
☐ Evening

In addition to the times above, some shops in busier resorts stay open until later in the evening and open on Sunday. Department stores are open 10–8. Some shops (including pharmacies) close Saturday afternoon.

Bank winter opening times are 8–3 (Saturday until 1PM). Banks are closed Sunday all year. The opening times of museums is variable; some close Saturday afternoon and all day Sunday, others on Monday (or another weekday), while some remain open all week.

DRIVE ON THE
RIGHT

TOILETS

PUBLIC TRANSPORT

Internal-Island Flights All of the Canary Islands have an airport and are inter-connected by air. The main operators are Binter Canarias (☎ 902 39 13 92), Aviaco (☎ 902 40 05 00) and Air Europa (☎ 928 57 95 84). Flight times are around 30 minutes. Flights between Gran Canaria and Tenerife are almost hourly. Inter-island flights are well used by islanders and early booking is essential.

Buses Global Salcai Utinsa operate these buses (☎ 902 38 11 10). Services, including express, run from Las Palmas to resorts in the south and to many towns and villages in the centre and the north. Services are reasonably frequent and start from the bus station at Parque San Telmo (☎ 928 36 83 35). Always check bus numbers used in this guide before making your journey.

Internal-Island Ferries All of the Canary Islands can be reached by ferry, mostly run by Trasmediterránea (☎ 902 45 46 45), departing daily from Puerto de la Luz in Puerto de Las Palmas. There is also a regular jetfoil/hydrofoil service ARMAS (☎ 928 30 06 00) between Las Palmas (Gran Canaria) and Santa Cruz (Tenerife) – 100 minutes – and Morro Jable (Fuerteventura). Fred Olsen (☎ 928 49 50 40) runs ferries daily from Puerto de Las Nieves (Agaete) to Santa Cruz.

Urban Transport In Las Palmas, the Guaguas Municipales (city bus service) runs three routes (1, 2, 3) leaving from the Bus Station Square, the Plaza de Cairasco or General Franco, depending on their destination. City suburb services start from the Plaza del Mercado. Smaller towns such as Telde, Santa Lucía, Arucas, Santa María de Guía and Gáldar have their own buses.

CAR RENTAL

There are plenty of car-hire firms, usually offering unlimited mileage. Prices vary considerably between large hire companies and small local firms; shop around, keeping in mind that this may reflect genuinely competitive rates or hazardous corner-cutting in maintenance.

TAXIS

Taxis are identified by the letters SP (*servicio público*) on the front and rear bumpers. Most are metered at a rate fixed by the municipal authorities. For short trips in tourist areas the meter will normally be switched off. There are usually fixed rates for long distances.

DRIVING

Speed limits on motorways (*autopista*) and *autovias*: **120kph**

Speed limits on country roads: **90kph.** Speed limits on urban roads: **50kph**

Speed limits in residential areas: **20kph**

Must be worn in front seats at all times and in rear seats where fitted.

Random breath-testing. Never drive under the influence of alcohol.

Fuel (*gasolina*) is sold as *Sin plomo* (unleaded) and *Gasoleo* (diesel). Petrol stations are relatively numerous along main roads with 24-hour opening in the larger resorts and towns, though some only open until 2PM on Sunday. In the mountains there are few, if any, filling stations and the steep winding roads are very thirsty, so fill up first.

If you break down in your own car the Royal Automobile Club of Gran Canaria, Léon y Castillo 279 (☎ 928 23 07 88), can offer advice on breakdown and repair services. Repairs are usually dealt with promptly. If the car is hired, telephone the local office of the firm and be sure to follow the instructions given in your rental documentation.

Ruler scale

```
CENTIMETRES  0  1  2  3  4  5  6  7  8
INCHES       0        1        2        3
```

PERSONAL SAFETY

Violence against tourists is unusual. Theft from cars is the most common form of crime, particularly in Las Palmas. There are three police forces: Policía Municipal (blue uniforms), Policía Nacional (brown uniforms) and Guardia Civil (pea-green uniforms). To help them and yourselves:

● Do not leave valuables on the beach or poolside.

● Leave valuables in hotel safe deposit boxes.

● Never leave anything of value in your car.

● Avoid the seamier streets of Las Palmas at night.

Police assistance:
☎ **112**
from any call box

TELEPHONES

Light-blue public telephone booths (*Cabina de Teléfono*) are the cheapest to call from. Most take coins, credit cards or a phonecard (*credifone*) available from post offices and some shops. Or use a *telefónica* cabin where the phone is metered and you pay after your call.

International Dialling Codes

From Gran Canaria to:	
UK:	**00 44**
Germany:	**00 49**
USA:	**00 1**
Netherlands:	**00 31**

Mainland Spain: full nine-digit number

POST

Post Offices
Post boxes are yellow. Use the slot marked *extranjero* (foreign) for postcards home. Post offices (*correos*) sell stamps (*sellos* or *timbres*) and provide telegram and fax services. Open: 8:30–8:30 (9:30–2 Sat). Closed: Sun

ELECTRICITY

The power supply is: 220 volts (older buildings: 110 volts)

Sockets take two-round-pin continental-style plugs.

Visitors from the UK require an adaptor and US visitors a voltage transformer. Power cuts are not infrequent, so pack a torch.

TIPS/GRATUITIES

Yes ✓ No ✗		
Restaurants (if service not included)	✓	10%
Cafés/bars	✓	loose change
Taxis	✓	10%
Porters	✓	€1–€2/bag
Chambermaids	✓	€1–€2/week
Cloakroom attendants	✓	loose change
Hairdressers	✓	10%
Theatre/cinema usherettes	✓	loose change
Toilets	✗	

PHOTOGRAPHY

What to photograph: wildly varied scenery from the rugged volcanic cliffs and mountain ridges of the western side of the island to the desert-like dunes of Maspalomas in the south.

Restrictions: it is forbidden to take photographs of military bases, military or naval port areas, police, government or military personnel, and inside museums.

Buying film: all popular brands and types of film, as well as camera and flash batteries, are readily available and reasonably priced.

HEALTH

Insurance

Nationals of the EU and certain other countries receive free medical treatment in the Canaries with the relevant documentation (EHIC – European Health Insurance Card for UK nationals), although private medical insurance is still advised and essential for all other visitors.

Dental Services

Dental treatment has to be paid for by all visitors. There are many English-speaking dentists; your hotel or tourist information centre will inform you of the nearest one. Private medical insurance will cover emergency dental costs.

Sun Advice

The south of the island experiences virtual year-round sunshine. The sun is at its strongest in the summer months when precautions should be taken. The north of the island is ofter cooler with cloud to filter the sun's harmful rays.

Drugs

Prescription and non-prescription drugs and medicines are available from pharmacies (*farmacias*), distinguished by a large green cross. They are able to dispense many drugs which would be available only on prescription in other countries.

Safe Water

Tap water is generally safe but is not recommended for its taste. Anywhere, but especially outside tourist resorts, it is advisable to drink bottled water (*agua mineral*), sold either *sin gaz* (still) or *con gaz* (carbonated).

CONCESSIONS

Students and Youths For various reasons Gran Canaria and the other Canary Islands do not attract backpacking youngsters the same way as other holiday islands throughout the world. There are only two youth hostels (*albergues*) and only two official campsites on the island. There are few, if any, student or youth concessions available.

Senior Citizens Gran Canaria is an excellent destination for older travellers, especially in winter when the climate is ideal. Some hotels offer long-stay discounts. The best deals are available through tour operators who specialise in holidays for senior citizens.

CLOTHING SIZES

Gran Canaria	UK	Rest of Europe	USA		
46	36	46	36		
48	38	48	38		
50	40	50	40		Suits
52	42	52	42		
54	44	54	44		
56	46	56	46		
41	7	41	8		
42	7½	42	8½		
43	8½	43	9½		Shoes
44	9½	44	10½		
45	10½	45	11½		
46	11	46	12		
37	14½	37	14½		
38	15	38	15		
39/40	15½	39/40	15½		Shirts
41	16	41	16		
42	16½	42	16½		
43	17	43	17		
34	8	34	6		
36	10	36	8		
38	12	38	10		
40	14	40	12		Dresses
42	16	42	14		
44	18	44	16		
38	4½	38	6		
38	5	38	6½		
39	5½	39	7		Shoes
39	6	39	7½		
40	6½	40	8		
41	7	41	8½		

WHEN DEPARTING

- Remember to contact the airport on the day prior to leaving to ensure the flight details are unchanged.
- If travelling by ferry you must check in no later than the time specified on the ticket.
- Although there is no restriction on the amounts of alcohol and tobacco you may bring into the Canary Islands, you must comply with the import restrictions of the country you are travelling to (check before departure).

LANGUAGE

Canary Islanders speak Castilian (the language of Mainland Spain). The only difference is in the pronunciation. Islanders don't lisp the letters 'c' or 'z', they are spoken softly. They also speak with a slight lilt, reminiscent of the Caribbean. There are a few indigenous words still in use, the most notable being *guagua* (pronounced wah-wah) meaning bus, and *papa*, meaning potato. In major resorts English is widely spoken but off the beaten track a smattering of Spanish is helpful.

Below is a list of some useful words. More extensive coverage can be found in the AA's *Essential Spanish Phrase Book* which lists over 2,000 phrases and 2,000 words.

hotel	*hotel*	breakfast	*desayuno*
room	*habitación*	toilet	*lavabo*
single/double	*individual/doble*	bath	*baño*
one/two nights	*una/dos noche(s)*	shower	*ducha*
per person/per room	*por persona/por habitación*	en suite	*en su habitación*
		balcony	*balcón*
reservation	*reserva*	key	*llave*
rate	*precio*	chambermaid	*camarera*

bank	*banco*	change money	*cambia dinero*
exchange office	*oficina de cambio*	bank card	*tarjeta del banco*
post office	*correos*	credit card	*tarjeta de crédito*
cashier	*cajero*	giro bank card	*tarjeta de la caja postal*
money	*dinero*		
coin	*moneda*	cheque	*cheque*
foreign currency	*moneda extranjera*	traveller's cheque	*cheque de viajero*

restaurant	*restaurante*	snack	*merienda*
bar	*barra*	starter	*primero plato*
table	*mesa*	dish	*plato*
menu	*carta*	main course	*plato principale*
tourist menu	*menú turístico*	dessert	*postre*
wine list	*carta de vinos*	drink	*beber algo*
lunch	*almuerzon*	waiter	*camarero*
dinner	*cena*	bill	*cuenta*

aeroplane	*avión*	port	*puerto*
airport	*aeropuerto*	ticket	*billete*
flight	*vuelo*	single/return	*ida/ida y vuelta*
bus	*guagua*	timetable	*horario*
bus station	*estación de guagua*	seat	*asiento*
		free	*libre*
bus stop	*parada de guagua*	reserved	*reservado*
		non-smoking	*no fumadores*
ferry	*transbordador*		

yes	*sí*	help!	*ayuda!*
no	*no*	today	*hoy*
please	*por favor*	tomorrow	*mañana*
thank you	*gracias*	yesterday	*ayer*
hello	*hola*	how much?	*cuánto*
goodbye	*adiós*	expensive	*caro*
good night	*buenas noches*	open	*abierto*
excuse me	*perdóneme*	closed	*cerrado*

125

INDEX

Acknowledgements

The Automobile Association wishes to thank the following photographers and associations for their assistance in the preparation of this book:
MARY EVANS PICTURE LIBRARY 10, 11b, 14; SPECTRUM COLOUR LIBRARY 9a, 11a, 51b, 93b; www.euro.ecb.int/ 119 (euro notes).
The remaining photographs are held in the Association's own library (AA WORLD TRAVEL LIBRARY) and were taken by:
J EDMANSON 59a; E MEACHER 58, 58c; A MOLYNEAUX 59b; C SAWYER Front cover, 5b, 6, 7a, 7b, 13a, 15b, 17, 18, 23, 24, 25, 26, 36, 39, 44, 49, 51a, 54, 55, 57, 67, 68, 69, 70, 74, 75, 76, 77, 82, 83, 87, 88, 117a, 117b; JA TIMS 1, 2, 5a, 8, 9b, 12, 13b, 16, 19, 20, 20/1, 22, 27a, 27b, 31a, 32, 33, 40, 41, 42, 43, 45, 46, 47, 48, 50, 52, 53, 56, 60, 62, 63, 64, 65, 66, 71, 72, 73, 78, 78/9, 80, 81, 84, 85, 86, 90, 93a, 122a, 122b, 122c.

Updated by Andrew Sanger

Dear Essential Traveller

Your comments, opinions and recommendations are very important to us. So please help us to improve our travel guides by taking a few minutes to complete this simple questionnaire.

You do not need a stamp (unless posted outside the UK). If you do not want to cut this page from your guide, then photocopy it or write your answers on a plain sheet of paper.

Send to: **The Editor, AA World Travel Guides, FREEPOST SCE 4598, Basingstoke RG21 4GY.**

Your recommendations…

We always encourage readers' recommendations for restaurants, nightlife or shopping – if your recommendation is used in the next edition of the guide, we will send you a *FREE* AA *Essential* Guide of your choice. Please state below the establishment name, location and your reasons for recommending it.

_____
_____
_____
_____

Please send me **AA *Essential*** _____

About this guide…

Which title did you buy?
    AA *Essential* _____
Where did you buy it? _____
When? m m / y y

Why did you choose an AA *Essential* Guide? _____
_____
_____
_____
_____

Did this guide meet your expectations?
    Exceeded ☐ Met all ☐ Met most ☐ Fell below ☐
    Please give your reasons _____
_____
_____
_____

continued on next page…

Were there any aspects of this guide that you particularly liked? _____

_____

_____

Is there anything we could have done better? _____

_____

_____

About you...

Name (*Mr/Mrs/Ms*) _____

Address _____

_____

_____ Postcode _____

Daytime tel nos _____

Please only give us your mobile phone number if you wish to hear from us
about other products and services from the AA and partners by text or mms.

Which age group are you in?
Under 25 ☐ 25–34 ☐ 35–44 ☐ 45–54 ☐ 55–64 ☐ 65+ ☐

How many trips do you make a year?
Less than one ☐ One ☐ Two ☐ Three or more ☐

Are you an AA member? Yes ☐ No ☐

About your trip...

When did you book? m m / y y   When did you travel? m m / y y
How long did you stay? _____
Was it for business or leisure? _____
Did you buy any other travel guides for your trip?
    If yes, which ones? _____

Thank you for taking the time to complete this questionnaire. Please send it to us as soon as
possible, and remember, you do not need a stamp (*unless posted outside the UK*).

Happy Holidays!

The information we hold about you will be used to provide the products and services requested
and for identification, account administration, analysis, and fraud/loss prevention purposes. More
details about how that information is used is in our privacy statement, which you'll find under the
heading "Personal Information" in our terms and conditions and on our website: www.theAA.com.
Copies are also available from us by post, by contacting the Data Protection Manager at AA,
Fanum House, Basing View, Basingstoke, Hampshire, RG21 4EA.

We may want to contact you about other products and services provided by us, or our partners (by
mail, telephone) but please tick the box if you DO NOT wish to hear about such products and
services from us by mail or telephone. ☐